A God of Incredible Surprises

Celebrating Faith
Explorations in Latino Spirituality and Theology
Series Editor: Virgil P. Elizondo

This series will present seminal, insightful, and inspirational works drawing on the experiences of Christians in the Latino traditions. Books in this series will explore topics such as the roots of a Mexican American understanding of God's presence in the life of the people, the perduring influence of the Guadalupe event, the spirituality of immigrants, and the role of popular religion in teaching and living the faith.

The Way of the Cross: The Passion of Christ in the Americas
    edited by Virgil P. Elizondo
Faith Formation and Popular Religion: Lessons from Tejano Experience
    by Anita De Luna
Border of Death, Valley of Life: An Immigrant Journey of Heart and Spirit
    by Daniel G. Groody
Mexican Spirituality: Its Sources and Mission in the Earliest Guadalupan Sermons
    by Francisco Raymond Schulte
The Virgin of Guadalupe: Theological Reflections of an Anglo-Lutheran Liturgist
    by Maxwell E. Johnson

A God of Incredible Surprises

Jesus of Galilee

Virgilio Elizondo

ROWMAN & LITTLEFIELD PUBLISHERS, INC.
Lanham • Boulder • New York • Oxford

ROWMAN & LITTLEFIELD PUBLISHERS, INC.

Published in the United States of America
by Rowman & Littlefield Publishers, Inc.
A wholly owned subsidiary of the Rowman & Littlefield Publishing Group, Inc.
4501 Forbes Boulevard, Suite 200, Lanham, Maryland 20706
www.rowmanlittlefield.com

PO Box 317
Oxford
OX2 9RU, UK

British Library Cataloguing in Publication Information Available

Library of Congress Cataloging-in-Publication Data

Elizondo, Virgilio P.
  A God of incredible surprises : Jesus of Galilee / Virgilio Elizondo.
    p. cm. — (Celebrating faith)
Includes bibliographical references and index.
  ISBN 0-7425-3388-3
  1. Jesus Christ—Person and offices. I. Title. II. Series.
  BT203.E53 2003
  232—dc21

                                2003013519

Printed in the United States of America

∞™ The paper used in this publication meets the minimum requirements of
American National Standard for Information Sciences—Permanence of Paper
for Printed Library Materials, ANSI/NISO Z39.48-1992.

To my family, friends, colleagues,
and
the people I have been privileged to serve
In my forty years of parish ministry in Texas:

Our Lady of Sorrows, San Antonio
St. Mary's, Stockdale
Sacred Heart, Floresville
San Fernando Cathedral, San Antonio
St. Rose of Lima, San Antonio

~

Contents

~

Acknowledgments

I begin with profound gratitude to the loving God into whose mystery I have entered in a very personal way through my lifetime friendship with *Jesús Nazareno* and *la Virgen María*. It is they who have brought out the unsuspected meaning of life with its many struggles, tribulations, joys, and *fiestas*.

This book could have never come about without the constant support, inspiration, encouragement and wisdom of many people—some whose name I do not even know, while others are among my closest friends! First of all, the memory of my grandparents and parents continues to be a great source of strength and wisdom. My sister Anita and her husband Mario Valencia together with my nieces and nephews and their children: Marisa; Monica, Paul, and Mariel; Esther, Andrew, Sarah, and Julian; James, Tara, and Antonio Cruz; and Robert and Kimberly have always been a great source of love and support. The dedication and compassion of my archbishop, Patrick F. Flores, of the clergy and religious of my archdiocese, and of great colleagues like Bishop James Folts of the Episcopal Diocese of West Texas, Pastor Buckner Fanning of Trinity Baptist Church, and Rabbi Samuel Stahl of Temple Bethel continue to be a living experience of the God's unlimited and unconditional love.

Many of the experiences narrated in this book come from my boyhood experiences in Christ the King parish and from the people of the parishes I have served. The pastoral institutes, universities, and dioceses where I have taught have given me the opportunity to enter into enriching conversations with the participants. Many of their insights have become part of this book. The great work of the scholars whose books and articles I have been able to study has been illuminating, instructive, and challenging. I am especially grateful for the abundance in recent times of critical studies carried out by great scholars on the historical reality of Galilee. I could have never accomplished this work without their marvelous insights. The variety of their scholarly opinions has been provocative and exciting. They became great conversation partners, and their works appear in the bibliography.

The theological reflection team of the Mexican American Cultural Center has constantly listened to the voices of the people, discerning the presence of God in their struggles for dignity and belonging through the study of the scriptures and proclaiming the biblical wealth of our Latino traditions and celebrations of faith. In particular I am indebted to my scripture consultants John Linskens, CICM, Juan Alfaro, and Juan Mateos, SJ; to "barrio experts" Roberto Pina, Ruben Alfaro, and Leonard Anguiano; to the pastoralists Maria Elena Gonzalez, RSM, Rosendo Urabazzo, CMF, Jane Hotstream, RSM, Dolorita Martinez, OP, Vincent Lopez, OCarm, and Rudy Vela, SM; liturgists Casiano Floristan, Luis Maldonado, and Rosa Maria Icaza, CCVI; linguists Sylvia Sedillo and Ricardo Jimenez; catechists Anita de Luna, MCDP, and Angela Erevia, MCDP; theologians Jacques Audinet, Raymond Brodeur, Dorothy Folliard, OP, Gustavo Gutierrez, OP, Leonardo Boff, Jose Oscar Beozzo, and Bill Wyndale, CICM, musician Carlos Rosas, and artist Consuelo Pacheco, DC. These are but a few of the many people who across the years have been part of MACC's "teología y pastoral de conjunto" team.

The creative and dedicated team of Catholic Television of San Antonio under the leadership of Ronnie Perez have taught me the logic of visual language and its importance in communication. This has been extremely useful in reflecting on the image message of the scriptures. The parish of St. Rose of Lima where I now serve as vicar is a marvelous example of the Christian communities of Apostolic times. The pastor, Father Juan Alfaro, truly believes that the people are the Church! It is a very multiethnic parish where anyone who comes to worship with us comments on the great love and joy they experience with us. It is truly a place made sacred because of its welcoming and caring spirit for anyone and everyone.

My friends, colleagues, and students at the University of Notre Dame and in particular in the Department of Theology and the Institute for Latino Studies are a great source of information, knowledge, and wisdom. It is a marvelous community of friends and colleagues who work, play, and pray together. I am grateful to my students who have given me valuable insights, especially Penny Wolf, Justin Campbell, Edward Hernandez, and Jason McMahon. I am especially grateful to professors John Cavadini, Gustavo Gutierrez, OP, Robert Krieg, and Mark Doak for their reviews and comments on this work. Professors Timothy Matovina and Daniel Groody, CSC, have been patiently accompanying me for several years as this work went through various phases, encouraging me and offering critical and valuable suggestions. The heart-rendering experience of Daniel with the Latin Americans trying to come into the United States for work has deepened and expanded my awareness of the power of faith and hope for survival against the most death-bearing circumstances; they risk hardships and death because of their love for their families! Much of Tim and Dan's wisdom is woven throughout this book and their friendship is a constant source of strength.

The inspiration and support of the Institute for Latino Studies has been without measure. The vision of director-professor Gilberto Cardenas is challenging and exciting. The friendship and support of the entire team is marvelous. I am especially grateful for assistance in bringing this book to completion to Maria Teresa Garza, Anthony Suarez, and Marisa Marquez. Their expert assistance in offering critical suggestions, putting the bibliographies together, researching specific points, checking scripture references, proofreading, and doing anything else that needed to be done brought this project to a beautiful completion.

Other colleagues whose friendship and comments have been most helpful include Maria Pilar Aquino of the University of San Diego, Alejandro Garcia-Rivera of the Jesuit School of Theology in Berkeley, Eilish Ryan, CCVI, of the Pastoral Institute of the University of the Incarnate Word, David Carrasco of Harvard Divinity School, Roberto Goizueta of Boston College, Timothy Scully, CSC, Richard Warner, CSC, Michael Lee and Natalia Imperatori-Lee of Notre Dame, Maria Elena Gonzales and Janie Dillard of the Mexican American Cultural Center, David Garcia, Felipa Peña, Joann Montez, and Mary Esther Bernal of San Fernando Cathedral.

Since his first reading of the manuscript, my most enthusiastic supporter and critic has been my very good friend Jim Langford—a professional of great wisdom, compassion, and vision. I also want to thank Andy Brozyna for the beautiful cover design and Lynn Weber for the great editorial work on this book.

Finally, I am most grateful for the love and support of my many friends—people of various races, ethnicities, religions, and social classes. In every one I have met, I have experienced a bit more of God's infinite goodness, beauty, and love.

CHAPTER ONE

~

A Family Friend

"I have called you friends"—*John 15:15*

I grew up in the Mexican tradition of Christianity, which is based on two principal icons: *Jesús Nazareno*, suffering for us on the cross and with us in our struggles; and *Nuestra Señora de Guadalupe*, reigning majestically in the temple of our hearts while offering us all her love, defense, and protection. They never appeared as doctrines to be believed or abstract truths to be memorized, but as beloved persons to converse with as they walked with us on the journey of life. From my earliest childhood I grew up with the assurance that I could place complete confidence in them, for they would never fail me, deceive me, or abandon me. I grew up knowing that in them and through them I would find responses to the many questions and enigmas of life. After a long life and many studies in various disciplines, I have no reason to begin doubting this today. I have reflected a lot and written a little on both Our Lady of Guadalupe and the Galilean Jesus, but now I want to probe deeper into the mystery and gift of the Word made flesh who walks among us today—a series of the most incredible surprises anyone would ever dare to imagine.

In our *barrios*, we never heard anything about the Christological doctrines of the Church, but we knew Jesus of Galilee very well. From the earliest days of my life, I have known him as a close friend and companion. He was very present in the tabernacle as *Jesús Sacramentado*, and we easily and frequently visited with him as our most trusted confidant. Vivid images of him were found throughout our homes, barrios, and churches. Simple songs, like the *corridos* of our people, kept him alive among us. Ritual celebrations from the *Posadas* (Joseph and Mary seeking a place to stay where Jesus could be born), the *acostada del niño Dios* (the laying down of the "Baby God"), and the *levantada* (presentation of the Child Jesus) of February 2 to the vivid reenactments of *Semana Santa* (Holy Week) have kept the human Jesus very much present in our lives and communities.

From the baby in the crib or in the arms of his mother, to the one calming the fisherman on the boat, to the one feeding the multitudes or enjoying himself at table with all kinds of people, to the man washing the feet of others, to the man in deep agony in the garden, to the one scourged and crowned with thorns and crucified, the Jesus of the gospel narratives has been alive and well among us. On the cross he was no angelic figure or solemn high priest, but a beaten, bleeding, suffering human victim of injustice dying a painful death—just like people who have been and are victims of injustice. In his unimaginable weakness, humiliation, and apparent defeat, he empowered us to accept whatever came to us in life and to never give in. This very real and very carnal Jesus is my Savior. He is not a teaching of the Church, but one of our own in whom our own lives take on meaning. I have no problem with the Christological teachings of our Church, but the Jesus I know and seek to follow cannot be reduced to a mere doctrine anymore than you or I can be reduced to a mere definition about our identity. We are much more. The Jesus who accompanies us throughout our lives and suffers with us in our afflictions has been a tremendous source of strength in our culture. *Jesús Salvador* is such a popular figure among us that we often name our children *Jesús, Jesusita, Salvador, Encarnación, Cruz,* and other such names.

As much as we knew about Jesús Salvador, we were equally very aware of the destructive force of sin all around us. Even our games, like the *piñata*, made us aware of the presence of the deceiving devil. The piñatas were always made in the form of devils or wrecking balls with seven peaks (seven capital sins). We were blindfolded and given a rod to break the piñata. The lesson: in life the devil would come at us from many different directions and disguised in many different ways. It was our task to fight against evil so that the glory of God would come upon everyone. The prize was inside the piñata so no matter who broke it, the prize would be shared by all.

Unfortunately it wasn't only our games that made us aware of the presence of evil forces all around us. We knew of robbery, crime, cheating, vengeance, malicious lies, racial and ethnic slurs, beatings, humiliating insults, and even murder. But even more than that, we were well aware of the ugly prejudices people had against our African American neighbors and us. People called us ugly names, kept us out of many places because of our skin color, ridiculed us because of our accent, told us we could not make it in school or in society because we were not smart enough, and kept us out of seminaries and convents because we were not ethnically pure or holy enough to be there.

Our own were never present in positions of leadership in our Church, schools, or society—as if God himself did not trust us. We were to be docile servants of the dominant society. In our hearts we knew this was not right, and since many of the people who treated us as if we were inferior and unworthy apparently were good people, we could only attribute their ugliness toward us not as malice but as a result of a much deeper evil. In time I would come to recognize this deeper evil as structural sin, as structural violence, which leads "good people" to do bad and horrible things while being convinced they are doing good. It is this structural evil that distorts, confuses, and sometimes even perverts our image and appreciation of others, of God, and worst of all ourselves. It is this structural evil that blinds people from seeing the truth (Matthew 23:16–26, Catechism 399). Wasn't this exactly what happened to the good and holy people who condemned Jesus as diabolically possessed, as a blasphemer and a common criminal, while being convinced they were speaking for God? Wasn't this the very "sin of the world" (John 1:29) that Jesus came to demolish, the very structures of society that could not appreciate him and ultimately killed him? How did Jesus respond to all this? How does he respond today?

The quest to know this Jesús Salvador better, as I long to know my own close friends better, has been with me as far back as I can remember, but it has continued to intensify as I grow older. To know him simply as divine is no problem, for the divine will always be a mystery that is too far beyond us to fully comprehend; but to know him as a human being is a terrific adventure. One could never follow a purely divine Jesus, since we are not divine, but we could follow the human Jesus who came into our lives precisely to show us the way. Yet it is precisely in his humanity that his divinity is made manifest (Catechism 515) and in following his way our humanity becomes divinized. To many, Jesus of Nazareth will continue to be as much of a scandal as he was in his own time and for early Christianity. It was so difficult for the scandal of Jesus of Nazareth to be appreciated for what it truly was that St. Paul would dare to write: "And no one can say, 'Jesus is Lord,' except by the Holy Spirit" (1 Corinthians 12:3). Who really is Jesus the Galilean, and just why did God become such a man to reveal the heart and face of God to us?

The idea of continuing my reflections about Jesus of Galilee has been brewing in my mind and heart for several years but for some reason or another, I had not been moved to write about it, as if the theme needed more time to evolve and develop. It was while taking care of my slowly dying mother that I felt the energy to rekindle this project. It was as if her sleeping presence was giving me the inspiration and strength to get going.

Ever since the publication of *Galilean Journey: The Mexican American Promise* in 1983, friends of mine have been urging me to develop further the theme of the Galilean Jesus. How does Jesus of Galilee become the Christ to persons who feel doomed to exclusion and marginalization because of their mixed-race or mixed-ethnic origins? Why has he been such a strong salvific figure for the poor and marginalized of Latin America, especially in his final humiliation, suffering, and crucifixion? Is there something unsuspected in the humiliated Jesus that those of the dominant cultures have not detected? Is there something in the colonized identity of the Galilean that people who have never been colonized do not suspect? Is there something which the poor and exploited, the broken and humiliated, the ridiculed and separated of the world have perceived that the powerful of this world have missed? Has the human scandal of Jesus been too much, too ridiculous, too far-out for the good and nice people of this world—this world as structured by sin and injustice?

"The Spirit of truth, he will guide you to all truth"—John 16:13

Jaroslav Pelikan in his book *Jesus through the Centuries: His Place in the History of Culture* has demonstrated masterfully how different ages in different cultures have elaborated various images of Jesus that have allowed people of that space and time to recognize Jesus as their healer, as their liberator, and as their savior. Moreover, in seeking to write about Jesus of Galilee, each culture has in effect produced a self-image of their own ideal self. In seeking to know Jesus of Galilee they have come to know themselves, not as others say that they are, but as they truly are. This does not mean they have written a new gospel or merely adjusted the gospel to fit their needs, but that they discovered aspects of the gospel that others have not noticed or emphasized.

Because Jesus was born and raised in circumstances very similar to our own Mexican American experience, we truly encounter him and know him in a very personal way. And who can better understand us than those born and raised among us, or at least in similar circumstances. They have insights into us like nobody else. Such is the story of Jesus who was raised in Nazareth, a rural town in the multiethnic Roman colony of Galilee. As the French language so beautifully brings out, only when we can *connaitre*—be born with—can we know another. The verb "connaitre" in French, which means to know a person, is a combination of the roots for the words "with" and "born."

Because of the many struggles for identity and belonging in my own life, and as I have discovered, in the lives of other mixed-race persons of ethnic and racial minorities, the issue of the social perception of Jesus' earthly identity is of the greatest importance for us today. I have asked myself the question with greater and greater intensity: Just what man did God become? With what accent did he speak? Did he mix the various languages of his region the way we do today—a sort of "Aramgreek" like our own Spanglish? Did he have elegant mainstream speech? How was he regarded by mainstream society? What passport would he have carried, what visas would he have been denied? How would people have reacted to his looks and ethnicity? Because of the Incarnation, as John Paul II pointed out in his first encyclical, *Redemptor Hominis*, every detail of the life of Jesus is part of the revelation. The question keeps pounding within my head and in my heart: Who, humanly speaking, was Jesus of Nazareth, and why did God become this very particular, stereotypically marked human being in order to be the savior of the world? What is the saving element of his earthly identity? After all, God did not begin the salvation of humanity by belonging to the great conquering and colonizing empires of this world, but through the marginal poor of the colonized peoples of the world. Yet he did not convert the colonized into colonizers but allowed them to initiate something new that would go beyond the categories of colonizer-colonized.

"The truth will set you free"—*John 8:32*

The more I reflect upon the human Jesus of the Gospels, the more I discover how much he has to offer men and women of today who are struggling under the weight of low self-esteem, internalized notions of inadequacy, inferiority, and even ugliness. At the same time, others fail to appreciate the beauty and goodness of God because they stereotype others as ugly, inferior, and unwanted. It is amazing, especially among minorities, how often people think of themselves as less human, less deserving, less capable of achievement, and less beautiful than those of the dominant group. This low self-image along with the expectations that one will not do as well as the others are among the most destructive and oppressive elements that many people live with. It is this type of separating categorization of others that keeps people from entering into the unity of the human race intended by the Creator. This leads those who have been victimized by the sin of the world to commit the very destructive sin of not believing in themselves—as if God had created trash!

During my many years of teaching in various universities and especially during my work in San Fernando Cathedral, which is most of all a cathedral of the poor of San Antonio, I have become very aware how deeply the element of self-image and self-identity affects people's lives, conditions their social behavior, and limits or enhances their possibilities. Many students do not speak up in class discussions because of a deep inner fear that they know less than the other students or even that they are inferior to them. The fear is even more intense among students from oppressed minorities. They are often silent, not because they are not thinking but because they fear their manner of speaking might not be acceptable, beautiful enough to be listened to, or, even worse, that they have nothing of value to contribute. In fact, they usually have the most powerful insights to offer.

It has become increasingly evident over the years that one of the most demoralizing and enslaving factors in the lives of people of mixed race, or mixed ethnicities, is the constant feeling of "not belonging fully" to either one of the parent groups, of not being as beautiful as those of the dominant parent group. This engenders deep feelings of shame in one's looks, impurity of one's soul, unworthiness of one's being, and disregard for one's new cultural identity. Quite often, the beauty, creativity, and potential brought about by the new pool of genes (I would dare say cultural, linguistic, religious, and biological genes) that have come together in the *mestizo*, the person of mixed races, are not appreciated and are even disdained.

I have found that exposing mestizos and other marginal peoples to the Galilean Jesus has not only been very exciting but also very healing, liberating, and life giving. Out of his Galilean mixture, Jesus was able to transgress the segregating limits of purity of his people and begin a new universal fellowship that offered real hope to a humanity torn apart by tribal, ethnic, religious, and racial barriers. Closed identities lead to barriers of separation that are often, as it is evident today, the basis of hatred, gangs, enslavements, segregation, wars, and even holocausts. It is my growing conviction that the greatest thing Christianity has to offer the world is the Galilean Jesus who out of marginalization offers a new universal fellowship: a unity in diversity and a new humanity in the loving mixture of peoples. This is the Jesus who transgresses humanly made barriers of separation, no matter how sacred they appear to be, for the sake of human unity and who transgresses humanly created systems of purity of body and blood for the sake of the true purity of God: this is love beyond all limits. After all, are we not all invited to share in his own body and blood so that our own bodies and blood might no longer be a basis of separation and death? The resurrection is precisely the rising above the death-bearing segregating factors of the world. The risen body is no longer bound by the earthly stereotypes of race, ethnicity, class, or even clothing. Thus the risen Lord, as those that arise with him, is no longer this or that (in the limiting sense that this has functioned) but fully human, fully alive.

The human Jesus reveals both the lies of the world and the truth of God about human beings and even about the selfhood of God. It is true that Jesus reveals a very beautiful and loving God to us; but I think it is even more important and more revolutionary that Jesus reveals the truth, the good, and the beauty about us to ourselves and to others and in so doing reveals the true countenance and heart of God in whose image we have been created. He who was a scandal to the world from the very moment of his conception and who died condemned as a criminal is the greatest revelation of who is really a true, a good, and a beautiful human being. In him we discover the whole and life-giving truth about ourselves. In him, with him, and through him, we can disregard the stereotypes we have lived under and shout from our most innermost being: I AM! I am a true human being, a beautiful human being, a good human being—so much so that God was willing to send his son to give his life for me! It is amazing to me how in the midst of the most vulnerable moments in the life of Jesus and in his most scandalous actions, the deepest truths about our humanity and about God are revealed. As you accompany me through the following chapters, reflect upon your own experiences of suffering and struggle so that the truth of the Galilean may heal you, make you free, and bring you to the fullness of your humanity.

It is through the Galilean Jesus that shame is transformed into a new and triumphant life. No longer shame, but pride, gratitude, and even a sense of mission. No longer mere compliance to the dominant status quo, but a new creative spirit with new vision and values. As Pelikan wrote, "The way any particular age has depicted Jesus is often the key to the genius of that age" (Pelikan 1987, 3). In *nuestro amigo Jesús* a new humanity will emerge that will leave behind the destructive racial, ethnic, and religious barriers that destroyed so much of humanity in past generations and in many ways continue to do so today. This is indeed a new creation.

CHAPTER TWO

~

So Human, He Must Be Divine

**"And the word became flesh and made
his dwelling place among us"**—*John 1:14*

Isn't this an incredible affirmation? The eternal God became a determined and limited time. The infinite God became a very specific and particular space. The universal God became a culturally conditioned man. The all-powerful God became completely vulnerable in Jesus, the son of Mary, the man from Galilee. And what is even more incredible is that I and many others know him personally.

Because I believe Jesus of Nazareth to be my savior and acknowledge how, in many ways, he has been my healer and liberator (as I describe in *The Future Is Mestizo: Life Where Cultures Meet* [Elizondo 2000]), I want to know more about him as a human being; it is precisely through his humanity that he has redeemed our own humanity and has rehabilitated us to our original beauty and dignity as created in the image and likeness of God. My own church in its renewed interest in evangelization has emphasized the personal encounter with Jesus of Nazareth as the core of evangelization. But just who is this human being Jesus of Nazareth, and why did God become in Jesus the very particular and socially situated person that he

11

became? What is the salvific meaning of the very person that God became when God became flesh?

I remember quite well the great biblical scholar Luis Alonso Schökel, vice rector of the Pontifical Biblical Institute in Rome, saying, "Because throughout the Bible, and most of all through the Word made Flesh, God chose to reveal himself through the human, only to the degree that we appreciate the humanity of the Scriptures will we appreciate their divinity." So to probe the human dimension of the Scriptures is to probe the ways of God as revealed through the struggles of human beings to become fully human. The entire Bible is a witness of the revelation of a loving and caring God through the struggles of the enslaved for freedom, of the marginalized for inclusion, of the shamed for positive recognition, of the imprisoned for liberty, of the rejected for acceptance, of the nobodies to become somebody. Biblical revelation is about the God who hears the cries of the people, sees their suffering, and comes to save his people. The God of the Bible is the God of the struggles of humanity for freedom, dignity, and belonging (Exodus 3:7–8).

The amazing thing about our Christian faith is that we believe that it is through the humanity of Jesus that we come to know God personally. Brazilian theologian Leonardo Boff in *Jesus Christ Liberator* brings this out beautifully when he states that at the end of the nagging question about who Jesus of Nazareth really was, the early Christians finally arrived at the insight that he was so completely human, he must have been divine! Thus the human and everything about his human situation become essential elements of the revelation, essential constituents of the redemptive process (Catechism 515–518). I do not know of any religion that so respects and exalts the human as our Hellenistic-Judeo-Christian faith. In him, the true image of the human will be revealed. We are created to the image and likeness of God, but it is the man Jesus who is the definitive revelation of God and of the true humanity as created by God. In Jesus of Nazareth we discover the truth of God and the truth of the human—who God truly is and what it truly means to be a human being. No one human group or religion has an exclusive monopoly on the truth about God and about the human. In fact, as humans in search of absolutes, we quickly create idols! In his life and message, Jesus offers a synthesis of the most humanizing elements of the various ethnic traditions circulating in his home region of Galilee—the great circle of Gentiles. Out of Galilee, the land of the darkness, of ignorance, and the mixture of various peoples, will emerge the great light to all nations (Matthew 4:15–16). Another of God's surprises.

In our mestizo Christianity of Latin America, it is neither the defleshed images of a risen Christ nor the great Christological titles that appeal to the people, but the figures depicting the very human Jesus of Nazareth, whether as a baby, as a boy, or most especially as the man of sorrows. At no time is his divinity more apparent to us than during our popular rituals of Good Friday. It is in his very ability to endure suffering, even to the extreme of scourging, thorns, and crucifixion, that he best reveals his divinity. The ordinary Latino poor seem to have an inspired instinct allowing his divinity to shine through that which, according to our modern standards of greatness, success, and beauty, we would consider a failure and a disgrace.

In the last few years, many fine scholarly works on the historical Jesus, the earthly Jesus, the real Jesus, the Jewish and even the Greco-Roman Jesus have been written. I have studied all of them, have enjoyed them all, and have learned a tremendous amount about the culture, society, and religion of Jesus. The studies of these magnificent scholars have taken me a long way, but they all seem to fall short of asking the incarnational-theological question: Why did God become the very particular human flesh that God became in Jesus of Nazareth in Galilee in order to redeem humanity? It seems that these studies lead down a fascinating path but fall short of arriving at the core of the issue. Just what did this "redemptive incarnation" redeem humanity from? Why was it necessary precisely in the particular way that it happened? Why are the social and cultural details examined important to God's salvific process? What is their salvific value to men and women today? How do they make a difference in the lives of those who wish to follow in the steps of the Master, those who wish to follow The Way? These studies have definitely helped me to see and appreciate Jesus the Galilean in his sociocultural milieu, but it is the dehumanized poor people struggling to be recognized as human beings and allowed to belong to the human race that have led me to the theological insights regarding the salvific aspects of the marginal peasant from Galilee going out to invite everyone into the reign of God. Yes, he was a great miracle worker, teacher, and prophet, but there were others around. He could not be easily classified by their ordinary categories of judgment. So who was he? It is crucial to know not just that Jesus invited everyone into his company, but even more important who this Jesus was that was doing the inviting! To us today, he was the Son of God, but who was he to the people of his region and times? After all, it is not just what is said that is important, but who the person is who is saying it. What are his credentials? With what authority does he speak? Does he speak well and correctly?

Statements by important and well-recognized persons are listened to attentively while remarks by persons like Genoveva Martinez, the cafeteria cook, or Eusebio Perez, the undocumented immigrant, are easily ignored and even ridiculed, no matter how intelligent and profound they might be. The reputation or social status of the person who speaks is basic to the reception of any communication. People presuppose that words coming from a famous person will be important, while they usually don't even pay attention to the voices of those who are considered to be insignificant.

The gospel writers were not great scholars or academics but simply followers of Jesus who wrote for their own congregations out of what they remembered and tried to transmit to others (Catechism 515). They were not writing doctoral dissertations but memories of a person who had transformed their lives, of one who had given them a completely new way of perceiving themselves, others, and society. They were simply writing about the one who had opened their eyes to see in a new way, their minds to a new understanding, and most of all their hearts to love in ways previously unheard of (Luke 23: 13–53). They were very much like modern-day *Cursillis-tas* writing the memories of their *Cursillo* experience so as to communicate to others the joy and excitement of what they had experienced which had totally transformed their lives. (A Cursillo is an intensive, emotionally packed weekend experience that brings participants into a very personal encounter with Jesus as the Lord and savior of their lives. It often produces a very profound conversion and change of life in the participants.) They may not write with scholarly precision, but the depth of their thought shines through the very simplicity of their expression. They may not recount the experience of the Cursillo in the same way, but they are definitely speaking about the same Cursillo.

Jesus came into a world whose cultures, structures, values, priorities, ways of thinking, and even religions had been contaminated and deformed by sin. His own people had been enslaved, exiled, and colonized. They struggled with the many contradictions and conflicting tensions and aspirations of a colonized people. Should they fight for freedom? Should they simply assimilate to the more dominant and attractive Greco-Roman culture? Should they retreat to an ethnic enclave? There was another way no one else had thought about. Jesus did not come to put a bandage on a messed-up humanity but to initiate a totally new creation. And he would start his work through an identity and a social location that not even the devil, much less anyone else, would suspect anything good could come from! As the late biblical scholar Raymond Brown used to say, the God of the Bible is a God of incredible surprises.

"We have found the Messiah"—*John 21*

Since my earliest childhood, I have known *Jesús de Nazaret*. Still, appreciating the incredible ways in which he brings salvation to humanity continues to be a fabulous adventure. In seeking the divine meaning of the human events and circumstances that comes through the simplicity of the Jesus stories as recorded in the Gospels, I will make use of several sources that have helped me to appreciate in a very personal way just what Jesus was saving us from, what he was liberating us from. Since God became human so that through his humanity he could lead us to the divine, or as St. Augustine puts it, "God was born human so that we humans could be reborn divine," I will first of all try to read the Gospels as a human story that brings out aspects of our own human story, ones that we have not suspected or that because of sin, we do not want to hear. It is the human story of Jesus that illuminates our own story, revealing aspects of grace we had not suspected and sinfulness we had not recognized.

As a pastor of forty years, I will use some of the marvelous insights that I have gained over the years in gospel-reading groups with the Mexican American poor people of the great frontier between Mexico and the United States—the mestizo people of *la frontera*. I will also use the Jesús Nazareno who is alive in the popular traditions of the people. As one who loves art and who likes to contemplate God as the supreme and most creative artist, I want not just to read the Gospels but to try to look at the portraits of human reality that they present to us. I want to pay close attention to the picture presented by the words of the Gospels, for I believe that the gospel pictures put on living flesh to the realities presented by the words of the gospel stories.

As a Catholic I want to refer to the new catechism of the Catholic Church and other Church documents as an anchor to help me establish some basic points. These documents bring together the wisdom of many generations of searching. As a scholar, I will make use of the well-recognized critical works that have come out in recent times on the times, culture, society, religion, and philosophical trends of the time and land of Jesus. They have provided a fascinating invaluable stage-setting for reflections on Jesus of Nazareth.

Beyond all these marvelous sources, I have tried to rely deeply not on my own work but on the illuminating power of prayer and contemplation, for it is precisely in the silence before *El Santísimo* (the blessed sacrament), in the deep awareness of my own inadequacies in relation to the mystery of infinite love and wisdom, that the most beautiful insights have emerged, often too beautiful to find the words adequate to express them.

Finally, in reflecting upon some of the basic texts of the New Testament that have been especially powerful in my pastoral work, I want to state clearly what Third World, Afro-American, and feminist biblical scholars present as basic to all serious historical and theological Jesus research: the critical articulation of the author's social location and how this affects and determines the historical-theological reconstruction of Jesus. I study, work, and reflect theologically from within my lifetime experience of being a mestizo Mexican American living and working in the predominantly Mexican poor sections of my city of San Antonio and among the Latin American poor of the United States. As a child growing up speaking Spanish in the United States, I was often ridiculed and laughed at because of the way I spoke English. I often felt shame in the many demeaning ways in which the mainline society and even our religion portrayed us. We had to live with the many ugly stereotypes that were promulgated in the jokes, slurs, social studies textbooks, and media. Many of our people were kept out of public places and refused service because of the color of our skin. For a full presentation of my social location I suggest you read my autobiographical account in *The Future Is Mestizo: Life Where Cultures Meet* (Elizondo 2000).

"Emptied himself, taking the form of a servant"—*Philippians 2:7*

The more I read the New Testament narratives from the perspective of socially wounded men and women, the more I appreciate the words of Jesus: "No one has greater love than this: to lay down one's life for one's friends" (John 15:13). From his very conception, Jesus loved us so much that he totally laid down his life in many ways. He put aside all the prerogatives of his divine life and even of social life, so as to totally enter into the disfigurement, degradation, and suffering caused by the sin of the world.

In becoming human, the Son of God simply became one among the many (Philippians 2:6). We learn from Paul's first epistle to the Corinthians that most of the early Christians were not from the wise or well-born of this world. Studies on the first Christians bring out that they were mostly from the poor, servants, and disenfranchised of society. They who were considered nothing by the world, looked upon as the scum of society, found a new sense of dignity and fellowship in their fellow "nothing" who was now seen as the Lord of heaven and earth. God had installed as the Lord and savior of the world the very one who had been maligned and rejected by the builders of this world, by the powerful elites of society, and by the leaders of his religion. The rejected had become the founding stone of the new building.

In inspired hymns preceding any of the written pages of the New Testament, the first Christians joyfully and triumphantly proclaimed this fact. In what is considered one of the earliest inspired hymns of the Christian community (Philippians 2:6ff.), the true earthly identity of Jesus is proclaimed. So as to enter into flesh and blood solidarity with the victims of the sin of the world, that is, the slaves, servants, and "nobodies" of this world, he who was by nature of divine condition empties himself of all social rank and status and enters humanity in the form of a slave. The various English translations state "in the likeness of man." I personally prefer the translation of the *Nueva Biblia Española*, which, after stating that he took on the condition of a slave, states "he became one among so many"—in other words, one of the multitude of slaves and servants of the world, one of those without dignity and considered of inferior human condition by the dominant sector of society. The one who had freely humbled himself by being born among the nobodies was further humiliated by his scandalous death on the cross. Yet because of his obedient resolve to live his entire life in an entirely new way, totally different from the ways of sin, every knee would bend on the mention of his name and proclaim that Jesus Christ is Lord and the glory of God (Philippians 2:10–11). Only the power of love can defeat the powers of evil without introducing an even greater evil. Jesus was obedient until the bitter end to love humanity no matter the cost, no matter the sacrifice.

This "humiliation," which was recognized and proclaimed by the earliest followers of Jesus, is key to understanding how the life of Jesus functioned in a redeeming way from the very instant of his conception. The victims of sin are humiliated and ridiculed in various ways. They are robbed of their basic humanity. They are made to feel inferior and impure. Stereotypes are created to justify their subjugation, enslavement, and exploitation. They are often made to think that the only way to freedom and the fullness of human life is to become like the very people who have sinned against them. They think that the only way out of domination is to dominate others; the only way out of slavery is to enslave others; the only way out of exploitation is to exploit others; the only way to come out of inferiority it to make others inferior; the only way out of oppression is to become an oppressor. Thus the chain of sin is not broken, and evil continues to develop and spiral in the world.

In the man from Galilee, God becomes the exploited, inferior, impure, enslaved human being—not to approve of this condition and just make us feel good because we are crushed but to lead us out of this destructive spiral of evil. But neither is his message a call to arms and revolution, for that will only produce new forms of violence. He becomes the victim of sin to break the bondage of sin, and it is out of the victims, the "stones rejected by the builders," that the new creation, the true humanity, will come about.

God was born human so that we humans might be reborn divine.

—St. Augustine

~

CHAPTER THREE

Troublesome Beginnings

"But she [Mary] was greatly troubled"—*Luke 1:26–38*

The annunciation is one of the most cherished texts of the Christian tradition. I don't know of any gospel text, except the story of the birth and death of Jesus, that has inspired artists, musicians, poets, and school plays more than the Angel Gabriel announcing to Mary that she is to be the mother of the savior of the world in a manner totally unknown to her or to anyone else. We can even hear soft angelic music in our minds as we think of the beautiful artistry that has interpreted this text for us throughout the Christian tradition. It is indeed one of the great treasures of the life of Jesus. In Nazareth of Galilee the angel appeared to the young Galilean maiden to invite her to become the mother of Jesus, not through man but through the Holy Spirit. Terrific! But would anyone believe this?

This is the real beginning of the Jesus story—not just his ethnicity, social status, and religion but even the way he was conceived. It is interesting to note that the four women mentioned in Matthew's gospel account of the genealogy of Jesus are not the great mothers of Israel but women with some sort of irregularity and questionable status: Tamar, Rahab, Ruth, and the wife of Uriah. Is this giving us a hint about what is to come? So we can well ask the question: What healing and liberating news does this incident have to offer? What is the salvific signification of this fascinating beginning of the life of Jesus?

We all know this story well as narrated in the gospel according to Luke. An angel appeared to a young peasant virgin named Mary in her home in Nazareth, a very small town in Galilee, a very marginal region of the world. The angel announced to Mary that she would conceive of the Holy Spirit. She was fearful and reluctant because she did not know man. But the angel reassured her and she accepted. It is one of the most beautiful and moving stories of the gospel narratives and certainly one that has been re-created in art and music throughout the ages. The story appears so beautiful and so pure that it is easy to miss the radicality of the salvific truth that it contains. From the very onset we might easily ask: Who was going to believe her? Isn't it true that it is not who we are that we have to live with but who the people we live and work with say that we are? People have lost their reputations, their jobs, and even their lives not because of something they have done but because of what others have accused them of doing. A person's reputation can be ruined even by mere gossip or suspicion, even when these rumors are totally false.

I do not doubt for an instant the truth of this narrative as summarized in the Apostle's Creed: "He was conceived by the Holy Spirit, born of the virgin Mary." But I do ask myself what the redemptive value is for humanity of this affirmation. How does this respond to the mystery of evil? After all, to be conceived of the loving relationship of a man and a woman is not evil. It is the very opposite: the incarnation of love. Chaste sex is not evil, dirty, or wrong. A child born of this union is a blessing of God. So why should Jesus be conceived "of the Holy Spirit" and not through the sanctifying sexual relationship between Mary and Joseph? Did God make a mistake when in the very beginning God created man and woman to procreate new life together through their conjugal union? It is not as if God had to correct this original "mistake." To conceive new life in the context of love—I cannot think of anything more beautiful, pure, and holy! The embodiment of intimacy in matrimony was designed by the very holiness of the most pure God. There is no moment of human existence in which man and woman are more godlike than in the conjugal bond of love that creates new life, life to the very image and likeness of God. There is nothing impure or inferior of a child born from the conjugal union of husband and wife. So why would God want to begin in a different way when it came to the incarnation of God's own son?

Maybe we need to look for answers not in some kind of predestined angelic purity and exaltation but in the midst of the suffering caused by sin. After all, every aspect of the Christian message is about healing and rehabilitation.

In the creed, the affirmation "He was conceived by the Holy Spirit, born of the virgin Mary" is immediately followed by "he suffered under Pontius Pilate, was crucified, died, and was buried." The second affirmation has always been recognized as a scandal, even a curse (Galatians 3:13), while the first one has been presented as a beautiful, edifying, and angelic experience. Since the creed leaves out the entire life of Jesus and makes reference only to the beginning and the end of his life, I wonder if it is not indicating that both the conception and the death were part of the apparent scandal that would actually prove to be redemptive for humanity. Why would a social scandal be necessary to redeem humanity? Yet it was because the Word freely (Philippians 2:7) became this scandal produced by the sinful of the world that he would demolish their criteria of judgment and classification and thus be raised by God to be the Lord of heaven and earth—the most authentic norm of the truth of human beings.

Maybe I can get to what I want to say by sharing with you some pastoral experiences. I have counseled young and even older women who have been the victims of rape. They were totally innocent.

They were violently abused against their cries, protestations, and resistance. Yet they felt guilty, as if they had brought it about. They
were even accused of provoking the whole incident. Some felt so
deeply soiled that they were convinced they could never be clean
again. Even worse, a young girl was driven out of her home and
chastised by her brothers for having disgraced the family. In another
case that I dealt with, the brothers felt they had a sexual right to
their sister since she had already given in to another boy. That's not
the end of it. I have had several cases where the raped woman conceived. They were advised to have an abortion, but because of their
conviction that regardless of the way it happened, life is from God,
they refused. So the family disowned them and chased them away
from the home because they "had shamed the family." With insults
and threats they drove them away from their home and family. They
were left totally alone. The sinful men who had abused them, unfortunately sometimes even one of their own family, even a grand-
father, went along happily on their way while the abused woman
was ridiculed, shamed, ostracized, and branded in the depths of her
soul as impure and unworthy.

The rape of young women, even within their own household, is
especially prevalent among the poor of the world. Quite often, the
dominant feel they have a right to the sexual use of the bodies of
the dominated and quickly label them as promiscuous and sensual
in order to legitimize their abuse of them, as in the case of the soldiers of a conquering army who use the women and then leave them
behind with the babies they conceived. Often, once a poor woman
has been violated sexually she is ineligible for marriage, and many
times the only option open to her is prostitution.

And what would happen to the child born of rape or out of wedlock? You know the answer as well as I do. Sinful society has created
a dehumanizing lie to brand the product of its own sin. Common language even calls a horrible person by the same name we call a child
conceived out of wedlock: a bastard. The equation is obvious: the one
born out of wedlock is horrible! The child will be deprived of his or

her dignity as a human being by being labeled an illegitimate bastard. I have dealt with people who live in profound and painful abandonment because the man who fathered them has never acknowledged them as his children. Sometimes the legitimate children of this man ridicule and insult the half brother or sister the man has never given his name to. Jesus enters into solidarity with those suffering from this stigma by becoming himself one of them in the eyes of his society.

Hence it is no wonder that Jesus makes the basis of his life, identity, and mission the loving care of God as Abba—as his personal loving father, the ultimate father who alone really counts. How beautiful and life giving it is when an earthly loving father is a living icon of God's loving and merciful fatherhood. Yet when this is not there, God's loving fatherhood is still there. No human being is without a father, for God is the ultimate father of all, and without God, there is no life at all.

No one of us has chosen the way we were to be conceived, yet society classifies people according to the way they were conceived. I know that gender, race, class, and ethnicity are important in the sinful classification of persons, but even more basic is conception. Conception can become a curse and a scandal for the child if the father, who can easily remain anonymous, is a black in a dominant white society, or a Mexican in a dominant Anglo society, or a Gentile in a purist Jewish society. The mother cannot remain anonymous, but have you ever heard of an unwed father? It is the mother and the child who will suffer throughout their lives the stigma of "illegitimacy."

This is the deepest perversion of our sinful world: the victims are branded as impure sinners by the very sinners who victimized them! This brand seems to penetrate to the very depths of their being. This is the horrible perversion: the impure label the truly pure as impure and even convince them they are in fact impure and sinful.

"For nothing will be impossible for God"—*Luke 1:37*

So we come back to our story. In keeping with the statement of the Catechism, "there is not a single aspect of the Christian message that is not in part an answer to the question of evil" (Catechism 309). I have witnessed this in reading the annunciation text with victims of rape and sharing with them that the ever pure, holy virgin mother of Jesus went through a similar experience, and because God is more powerful, she remained a pure and holy virgin. Nothing is impossible with God. Thus she, like any other victim, remains pure and holy. She even remains a virgin, for the God who can resurrect his son from the dead can equally maintain a woman virginal even through the most horrible ordeal.

I believe that the redeeming scandal and sacrifice of Jesus started with his conception (Catechism 517). It happened in such an extraordinary way that I doubt if anyone would have believed Mary, even if they wanted to. People probably suspected everything else, even the worst, except what is recorded in the gospel narrative. Even the good Joseph was going to put her away. Quite possibly she was chased out of her home to avoid local scandal and for that reason went to stay with her far-off cousin. This "going away to visit a friend or relative" is quite common when people want to hide a pregnancy. She conceived and indeed it was of the Holy Spirit, for no life is conceived, no matter how much the parents try, without the Holy Spirit. All life is from God, and without God's will, there will be no life. In so conceiving in a way that would appear as scandalous or at least questionable to her contemporaries, Mary entered into flesh and soul solidarity with the suffering and loneliness of victimized women. She assumed an aspect of human suffering that Jesus as a man could never assume and thus began her role as co-redeemer.

What is rehabilitating to violated woman who are reflecting on the experience of Mary is to discover that regardless of what may have happened, Mary remained pure and unsoiled because God loved and protected her. Even if she had been abused by someone, she would not have lost her virginity because nothing is impossible with God. Virginity cannot be taken away; it can only be given. Even if she had been raped, by the power of God she remains the ever-virgin holy mother of Jesus. What the sinful world defiles, God maintains pure; what the sinful world prostitutes, God virginizes. The purity and dignity of a woman cannot be destroyed or harmed by the abuse of anyone, and God is there to heal the memories, rehabilitate wounded hearts, and restore ruined reputations.

In terms of our redemption, I believe the virginity of Mary is as powerful as the resurrection of Jesus because once someone's reputation is destroyed, even by suspicion, nobody but God can fully restore it. Virginity is God restoring a ruined reputation, God protecting the existential purity and holiness of the body, which no human being can destroy.

The cleansing and rehabilitating effect this saving truth has upon violated women is astounding. Prayerful reflection on this event keeps them from self-destructing in response to the feelings of impurity, unworthiness, and guilt that rape generated in them. If the power of God maintained Mary pure and virginal and worthy of being the mother of God, God will do likewise to anyone who puts their trust in God. For nothing is impossible with God.

"Decided to divorce her quietly"—*Matthew 1:19ff.*

How can any decent man marry a woman who has already been deflowered? Isn't this typical of the double standard of so many of our societies throughout history? The man can be as promiscuous as he wants, and in no way does this disqualify him for marriage or render him impure. In fact, sometimes young men are taken to prostitutes to be initiated and educated in the ways of making love; rather than a stigma, it is more something to brag about. But the woman is supposed to remain pure and virginal even to the point of proving her virginity during the first night of their wedded life. So Joseph here is acting like any normal male of his society. When he finds out that she is with child, he is going to get rid of her, in a quiet way, but nonetheless get rid of her. She would be left without the protection of a husband and with few job opportunities except that of prostitution.

It takes a divine communication through a dream for him to de-cide to take her as his wife. Yet the text does not seem to indicate that he had any tenderness with her since it states clearly: "He had no relations with her until she bore a son." I know that our Catholic tradition has always used this text to refer to the perma-nent virginity of Mary as something beautiful. I do not question this permanent virginity, but I wonder if this was not part of the ongoing suffering of Mary: the suffering of being rejected, of not re-ceiving the loving and tender gestures and touches that are sup-posed to be there in marriage. Not to receive the loving embrace of the one you love hurts deeply; it intensifies the feeling of unwor-thiness and impurity. In a home, it is horrible to feel tolerated but not wanted.

This was brought out to me very clearly during one of my Bible-reading sessions with people from the barrio. As we were studying this text, I extolled the virtues of Joseph, who went against social tradition and took her in as his wife. One of the groups had a dif-ferent reading of this text. "Yes, to a point Joseph was a hero, but he was equally cruel and insensitive. How horrible and lonely it must have been for Mary, the young and inexperienced girl, to just be taken into his home but for him not to have relations with her, not have anything to do with her. It must have really made her feel dirty and at best merely tolerated." I know scholars appreciate and value the technical explanations of these people, but the commonsense explanation of this reader, who perceived so much more in this text, cannot be discarded. I suspect it is very close to the truth of this text. This is consistent with the "scandal" reading of the various texts of the redemptive story of Jesus and with the absolute "empty-ing" of God to become "one among so many."

So once again, Mary enters into solidarity with the women who are taken in as wives only to cook, clean, do the dishes, clean house, bear children, and maintain the family without any trace of loving relationships between her and her husband. Such women are ser-vants without any of the benefits of servants. The solitude, loneliness, sense of being tolerated but undesired, and sense of insignificance and even impurity these women suffer are beyond words to describe. But they are not alone, because Mary is in solidarity with them, not to approve of the situation but to accompany them in their silent cries and tears so at least they do not suffer alone. There is at least one who truly appreciates their situation, is not ashamed of them, and reassures them of their fundamental dignity and worth.

"Most blessed are you among women"—*Luke 1:42ff.*

When we read the narrative about the conception of Jesus (Luke 1:26–38), we see fear, resignation, and acceptance but we do not find joy. In fact, the narrative ends in the stunned silence of Mary. It is not surprising. Even if the annunciation took place exactly the way it is narrated in the gospel account, we can well ask: Who was going to believe her? Some of the early detractors of the Jesus movement used this doubt about his conception to discredit Jesus. How could he be the Lord and savior of humanity if he was illegitimate (Catechism 498)? This was something so out of the ordinary that we can be sure that no one was going to believe her. Even the ones who loved her the most and knew her well were bound to beg her to tell them what really happened.

Furthermore, thinking of the consequences must have been most frightful: Was she going to be abandoned with her child? Would there be anyone to protect her? Would she be banished from the family? Punished publicly? Stoned to death? I have dealt with similar fears with women who find themselves pregnant out of wedlock. It is devastating.

But Mary goes to visit her cousin Elizabeth. When her cousin recognizes that what Mary carries within her womb is of God, immediately Mary rejoices and proclaims one of the most beautiful and powerful hymns found in the New Testament: "My soul proclaims the greatness of the Lord" (Luke 1:46). What others might look upon as a disgrace and a scandal, a baby out of wedlock, Elizabeth recognizes what every new life truly is: a gift of God! I have known of similar cases in which a violated woman was insulted in the most horrible terms by her own family as she was being driven from the family home, only to be taken in by a loving grandmother, aunt, or home for unwed mothers who rebuilt the dignity of the woman by welcoming her with kindness, treating her with dignity, praying with her, and assuring her that regardless of the circumstances of the beginning, rape or a mistake on her part, life is from God and that her child could be, as Jesus was, destined to be the savior of many people. I know one very good and effective priest today who came exactly out of these circumstances. His mother's family wanted her to have an abortion because she had conceived out of wedlock. At the last moment, she backed away and gave birth to a healthy child. The child became her life. He had difficulty being welcomed into a seminary because of his illegitimate status. Finally, he found a religious order that would accept him. He has accomplished wonders in his work as a priest.

No one fully understands the mysteries of God's ways, even in the conception of life. There is the normal way of conception, which is beautiful and holy, but even when conception has taken place in a different way, the child is still of God and a blessing for humanity. And the woman who conceived, even if she had been the most sinful of all, is still not rejected by God, for God rejects the sin but not the sinner. The sinner is not condemned but rather invited to experience the boundless mercy of a loving, understanding, and forgiving God.

In this sense, Elizabeth is the first one to proclaim the good news. Men (like Joseph) are scandalized, but women (like Elizabeth) understood and praised God. What had appeared to be a human story of pain and scandal, even to good Joseph, is now recognized and proclaimed for the great blessing that it truly is: "Most blessed are you among women and blessed is the fruit of your womb" (Luke 1:42). Thus it is not only the women who first proclaim the resurrection, but it is a woman who first recognizes the presence of God in the child in the womb of an unwed mother. It is the holiness of this woman that allows her to see reality for what it truly is: not a scandal but a great blessing. And the woman who others might be scandalized by is proclaimed for what every mother truly is: "Blessed." Every woman who is a carrier of new life is blessed, for during her pregnancy she is cooperating with God in a very special way in the creation of new life. It is the sinful eyes that cannot recognize life as a blessing and would not hesitate to get rid of the mother and the child. Yet the one who in her time was a scandal according to the sinful categories of judgment, would be called blessed by all generations to come who in the new creation began to see not as sinful humanity sees, but as God sees. Thus begins the scandalous good news of the new creation initiated by Mary and Jesus:

> For almighty God . . . because he is supremely good, would never allow any evil whatsoever to exist in his works if he were not so all-powerful and good as to cause good to emerge from evil itself
>
> —St. Augustine, Enchiridion 3, 11; PL 40, 236,
> as quoted in the Catechism 311

CHAPTER FOUR

~

Unsuspected Beauty

Among the Mexican people of San Antonio, the two most beautiful, attractive, and moving scenes of the year are the *pesebre
Navideño* and the *Viernes Santo*. The pesebre Navideño is no heavenly Christmas crib surrounded by angelic choirs, and the Viernes
Santo scenes are no sanitized liturgical versions of the original cruelty and bloodshed of the events of the first Good Friday. More and
more ethnic and social classes take part in these annual manifesta-
tions of the poor. They find something incredibly attractive in these
public rituals of a marginal birth and a shameful death that does not
appear to be present in their ordinary church services.

In one of the pre-Christmas *Posada* processions (in which participants walk through their neighborhoods for nine evenings, going
from home to home asking for shelter in a reenactment of the journey of Mary and Joseph to Bethlehem), I remember walking along-
side a group of young English-speaking persons. I got into a conversation with them and discovered that they were nuclear scientists
from the East Coast. One of them mentioned that as a tourist several years ago, he had just accidentally happened to be walking by,
had been curious, and had joined the procession. He had had such

a profound religious experience that now he returns every year just for this and brings some of his fellow scientists with him. This story is typical of many others I could recount. What attracts such people to these popular rituals that are not part of the official worship of any denomination?

These popular rituals surrounding the birth and death of Jesus present the stark, scandalous, and shocking realities of the original events as recorded in the gospel stories and remembered by the people. In many ways, they are so popular because they mirror the living reality of the people's lives and interpret it through the reenactment of God's entry into our lives through Jesus of Nazareth. We will return to the inner beauty of the apparent ugliness of Viernes Santo in a later chapter.

"No room for them"—*Luke 2:1–7*

The tradition of the posadas is a favorite ritual in the Southwest. The participants walk from house to house seeking shelter and are refused and driven away. Finally, after several attempts, one home welcomes the homeless group. The house that receives the pilgrims from Galilee is filled with joy, since it is in the reception of the homeless that God comes into our lives. For those who have often been refused services whether in restaurants, motels, public places, and even churches, this is a very significant ritual, for it reenacts ritually the reality of our lives and allows us to celebrate what we know well in our hearts but the ones who refuse us entry ignore: that we are not trash or contaminated problems to be kept out, but, like all human beings, blessings to be enjoyed.

In some ways, in going from Galilee, the land of much interethnic mixing, to Judea, with its fascination with Jewish purity, Joseph and Mary were like the immigrants who come from cultures we consider inferior into our "superior" U.S. culture or like people who have been conquered and colonized by a more powerful group. The people are welcomed as cheap labor to do the work none of the citizens are willing to do, but are distanced and kept away from the dominant population in many ways. Many have to sleep under bridges or in abandoned buildings because nobody will rent to them. It is not that there is no vacancy, but there is no room for them because of who they are.

This was probably the case for Joseph and Mary, who were despised Galileans seeking shelter in Judea. In this rejection, they enter into solidarity with the many immigrants who seek shelter in a foreign country only to be refused, again not because there is no room but because of who they are. So the emptying of God continues as his earthly parents are to be counted among the rejected of society so that he, too, will be born among the rejected of the world. Yet in the playful posada ritual reenactments of the people, the truth that is discovered by the shepherds is clearly recognized and celebrated: joy comes to the home that opens its doors to the homeless, for in receiving the poor and the marginal of the world we actually receive God. The final posada ends in the *acostada del niño* in the pesebre on Christmas Eve.

The whole Christmas story appears at once in the pesebre, including the visit of the Magi and the slaughter of the innocents. It is dressed up beautifully, but beneath the nostalgic beauty is the stark reality of a dismal situation. The shepherds are no charming princes, but dressed in rags and motley looking. The Roman soldiers look mean and cruel. The winter atmosphere with the snow and ice might be nice to observe from a warm fireplace but is definitely not good for a newborn child. It is a clear portrayal of the cruelty of life that is the daily lot of the poor and the unwanted; but in their faith in the God of life, they manage to rise above the oppressive forces and both see and celebrate the goodness and beauty of God and all of God's creation, especially in the birth of a child.

"Laid him in a manger"—*Luke 2:7*

What beauty could there ever be in a baby born in the dirty and messy stable, laid in a manger among the stink of animals because there was no room for them anywhere else, and then visited by lowly shepherds! Nobody had room for them because they were undesirables. In this deplorable situation "she gave birth to her firstborn son. She wrapped him in swaddling clothes and laid him in a manger, because there was no room for them in the inn" (Luke 2:7).

The manger is the place where animals come to feed. It looks bad, it smells bad, and there are usually plenty of mosquitoes and insects around to make life uncomfortable. There are no facilities or creature comforts whatsoever—no easy chairs, tables, or beds. That is why Joseph and Mary are portrayed kneeling around the manger: not in adoration but simply because that was the only way to be close to their newborn child. This position is quite normal among parents who are so poor that they have nowhere else to place the baby than on the ground of their huts. It is no proper place to lay a newborn child, unless you have absolutely nothing else. Society would consider this totally irresponsible. Yet this was the first manifestation of the God-made-human for us. It almost seems as if God had gone crazy! Abandoning his child to misery from the very beginning! This does not seem like a good, loving, and caring parent God.

It is this stark realism that the Mexican poor continue to present in their homes and barrios as beautiful and inspiring. And they are absolutely correct in doing so. "And this will be a sign for you: you will find an infant wrapped in swaddling clothes and lying in a manger" (Luke 2:12). There are many good scholarly interpretations of this text, but the faith-filled Mexican poor, who often have to give birth to their children in abject poverty and move from housing project to housing project because no one wants them around, see much more in the imagery of this text than I have gleaned from learned books.

"There is not a single aspect of the Christian message that is not in part an answer to the question of evil" (Catechism 309). The social location and circumstances of our Savior's birth were so totally out of sync with the world's standards of reason that, as the New Catechism of the Catholic Church points out, quoting St. Ignatius of Antioch, not even the devil could have suspected it (Catechism

498). In what way is the biblical imagery of the birth of Jesus an answer to the question of evil?

The great evil of the world, the structural sin of the world, is the destruction of human dignity, the denial of the beauty of the image of God that exists in every single human being, and the subsequent exploitation, marginalization, and exclusion that comes with it. Humanity in its sinfulness has created many ways of depriving individuals, peoples, and nations of their God-created dignity and sense of beauty and self-worth. Clothing, jewelry, property, money, housing, skin color, place of origin, family name, social position, and many other categories appear to define the truth and value of the human more than human existence itself. St. Augustine wrote that "nothing is more beautiful than truth itself." I would add, nothing is more beautiful, liberating, and life-giving than the truth about the human! This was so from the very beginning of human creation and was the great revelation in the very human that God became in Jesus. In the utter simplicity of the baby in the crib, without any externals or social status to distract our attention, the glory of God is made manifest. Indeed, it is the beginning of the good news for humanity.

In his opening address at the famous meeting of Latin American bishops at Puebla, Mexico, in 1979, John Paul II stated: "The truth we owe to human beings is, first and foremost, a truth about themselves." He goes on to state: "Perhaps one of the most glaring weaknesses of present-day civilization lies in an inadequate view of the human being. . . . Thanks to the Gospel, the Church possesses the truth about the human being."

The right-to-life movement is certainly correct in affirming the sanctity of life from conception to the grave. The tragedy is that while many struggle to defend the rights of the human in the womb, some of the same people totally disregard them once they are born. Most of our ways of categorizing human beings serve only to hide the ultimate truth of God: the glorious beauty and dignity of the human exists precisely because they are human—and as such they are nothing less than the image of God.

"Shepherds returned, glorifying and praising God"—*Luke 2:8–19*

God was born human among the homeless and rejected, born of a simple couple whom we know only as Mary and Joseph. It was the supposedly worthless and untrustworthy shepherds who first recognized the glory of God present in the baby in the crib. (In much of Hebrew literature, the shepherd was looked upon as quite heroic, yet in real life they were quite vilified—much like Mexican literature that glorified the ancient Nahuatl ancestors while vilifying the indigenous people today.) The message is clear, simple, and profound: In the nakedness of the baby in the manger, with none of the worldly trimmings that indicate dignity, nobility, aristocracy, or the like, the truth of God regarding the human is revealed. The human as human is the image of God and radiates the glorious beauty of God. In Jesus, God became the nothing of the world, so that the nothing and everyone else may know that no one, no one human being, is inferior to others. This is indeed "good news" for everyone, but especially for the "born-nothings" of this world.

One of the most beautiful and moving songs of the Mexican Christmas tradition is "*Vamos Pastores Vamos*," which celebrates the excitement of the shepherds going to Bethlehem to see the child who radiates the glory of heaven. It is a very festive song, sometimes even accompanied by dances as the shepherds approach the child in the crib. This song is very close to many of the people, especially since many of them are *campesinos*, often afraid of false offers of help and assistance. So many times offers of help turn out to be mere tricks to rob them. This night, they hear the call that, far from being afraid, they should be rejoicing, since a true savior has been born unto them.

The angels proclaimed to the shepherds: "Do not be afraid; for behold, I proclaim to you good news of great joy that will be for all the people. For today in the city of David a Savior has been born for you who is Messiah and Lord. And this will be a sign for you: you will find an infant wrapped in swaddling clothes and lying in a manger" (Luke 2:10–12).

It is amazing how easy it is for those who are not distracted by the glamour and the shining lights of pomp, commercials, and wealth to see the presence of God in the simple and the ordinary. I have often experienced this among parents and families whose faces radiate with divine joy when holding their own baby or the baby of one of their neighbors in their arms. There is no doubt in their minds that this baby is of God and that its purity and innocence reveal the very beauty of God. They need no rational, philosophical, theological, or ideological proof to establish the divinelike status of this baby. They have no doubts that this baby reflects the very beauty and image of God. I have become especially aware of this in baptisms of the poor at San Fernando Cathedral. The poor bring their babies to be baptized with such pride that there is no doubt they see in them a reflection of the divine beauty and dignity. As we baptize the babies, camera flashes go off as proud parents, relatives, and friends record this sacred moment. It is as if God was once again opening up the skies and saying about this baby: "You are my beloved Son, with you I am well pleased" (Luke 3:22).

The shepherds had absolutely nothing but their sheep, pastures, and the beauty of the skies. They were the outcasts of their society because they were considered to be cutthroats and impure, and quite probably because of the bad smell of the sheep, which became part of their own body smell. They were definitely not the ones who would be invited into polite society. They were considered impure persons whose word did not count. They did not need to go to a palace or basilica to find God. They did not need any miracles or biblical proofs that a savior had been born. They discovered the savior in the nakedness of a baby in a crib. Family name, clothes, and social status do not determine the dignity of a newborn child; rather by its very birth the child is a revelation of the grandeur and beauty of God.

But the symbolism of the Gospels goes much further. Caesar Augustus had ordered a census of the whole world. A simple statement, but an incredible affirmation. The building of the tower of Babel had now been completed. One man had now obtained divinity; "Augustus" means worthy of divine worship, recognized and acclaimed as such by all. He now had control and dominion of the whole world and thus could order a census—he could make use of everyone, their properties, and their monies for his own purposes. And the whole world had now become one city: Rome. He had power to take from the whole world whatever he wanted. The census was bad news for the entire Roman Empire.

In contrast to this, we have the nameless and homeless couple, Joseph and Mary, giving birth to an unknown child and placing him in a manger. And it is the outcasts of the world who recognize his birth. Another simple but fascinating affirmation. The all-powerful in contrast to the powerless; the census: I take from you to enrich myself, in contrast to the manger: the place where the flock comes to be nourished, the place that offers nourishment to all who come to it; the Caesar recognized as "Augustus" by the whole world in contrast to the nameless child in the manger recognized as the real savior of humanity by the outcasts of society. The "child in the manger" is indeed good news for humanity, for there is now a new measure of the ultimate dignity and worth of the human being: Our ability to live our lives in the service of others. The child in the manger is the very one who will give us his own body and blood as food for eternal life. Thus the bad news of the census in contrast to the good news of the manger.

This marks the beginning of the Messianic inversion of worldly values. Real human wealth is built up not by taking from others but by giving oneself to others. Real human dignity is revealed not by the social rank, titles, or status, nor by the fancy cloths or residence, nor by the family name one bears but simply by the fact that one is human. The all-powerful name of Caesar Augustus has faded into the dusty volumes of history books, while the memory of the then-nameless and unknown Joseph, Mary, and Jesus is known and celebrated the world over! The ways of God are indeed foolishness to the men and women of this world!

"For there is nothing hidden that will not become visible"—*Luke 8:17*

Sin has hidden what has been true from the very beginning of creation. Every human being is created to the image of God and is precious for those who see and recognize the truth of God's creation. This truth could not remain hidden any longer. Thus, to disregard anyone, to despise anyone, and even more to exploit, enslave, and rob the weak and the poor are offenses against the Creator. The natural order of human beings is not, as the Greeks and others thought, a society hierarchically structured by nature itself, some to be masters while others to be servants or slaves, some to be considered as civilized (themselves) and others (foreigners) as barbarians and savages. Even the Hebrew Scriptures considered some to be chosen and thus others to be rejected. This would not be the case for Jesus. Neither Greek nor Jewish thought and categories were sufficient for Jesus. Both had to be challenged and transcended in favor of the God of creation. For God, every man and every woman is created unique, different from others, but every single one is created with equal dignity, value, and beauty. They might have different responsibilities, but none is more valuable or more important than another.

Because sin divided humanity into "haves" and "have-nots," into beautiful and ugly, pure and impure, attractive and unattractive, powerful and powerless, important and discardable, nobility and commoners, welcomed and rejected . . . the grace of God in Jesus would come to destroy these sinful divisions. And in the wisdom and folly of God, this elimination of the divisions would come through the very victims of the world's sin. Joseph and Mary, traveling to a distant territory, are prototypes of the immigrant poor for whom "there is no room in the inn" of mainstream society. Mary and Joseph are among the rejected and despised poor whom nobody wants around. Yet out of this nameless and apparently worthless couple, the savior of humanity would be born. The one whom we most despise today might very well be our savior tomorrow.

The savior of humanity, the ultimate King of Kings, was not born in a palace or fancy home with luxurious surroundings but in the most simple and unassuming way possible—not because nice and comfortable things are bad, but because they have often deprived us of appreciating the basic value and dignity of the human by making us focus more on externals than on the intrinsic nature of human beings.

Yet through all this messy and apparently dehumanizing beginning, the glory of God would be revealed in the baby of Bethlehem. What could be more revealing of the beauty and majesty of God than the birth of a child? With each newborn child, the image and likeness of God are once again made visible. Or as our ancient Mesoamerican ancestors would say: Creation is once again renewed. The surroundings of the birth are insignificant in relation to the glorious beauty of God present in and through the child. No wonder the Mexican poor can pierce through and see glorious beauty in the stark reality of the manger. When all human and artificial masks of honor, prestige, status, and beauty are removed from human beings, the beauty of the glory of God's image shines through the human. As the new catechism puts it: "Jesus was born in a humble stable, into a poor family. Simple shepherds were the first witnesses to this event. In this poverty heaven's glory was made manifest. The Church never tires of singing the glory of this night" (Catechism 525).

In the stillness of the night, far away from any center of power or prestige, surrounded only by the beauty of the earth, the stars, the animals, and the most unassuming people of the world, God was born human! All the important persons and places of that moment have long been forgotten and even disappeared, but the power, the glory, and the life-giving force of the baby who had no place to be born continue to fascinate and inspire humanity throughout the world.

Who would suspect that anything of any importance would come out of this baby born of a homeless couple? But what is true of Jesus can be true of any human birth. Who can suspect what God has in store for any baby? The fascinating and hope-filled revelation of the infancy stories of Jesus is that, even if everyone considers a particular baby as insignificant or worthless, this very baby could be the one who is destined to save our lives. In each new birth, creation is renewed and there is hope for humanity.

CHAPTER FIVE

~

Where Are You From?

I travel a lot. Often when I meet people on the plane, one of the first questions we ask one another is "Where are you from?" Where we come from becomes an innermost element of our being and our identity. Our place of origin and citizenship has many important consequences. Visas can be obtained, delayed, or denied simply because of where we come from. Ethnic profiling can render one prey to police searches. People have definite, though often incorrect, ideas about people according to where they come from. In many ways it could be said that we are where we come from, and that identity renders us welcome, difficult to accept, or totally unacceptable. We can change in many ways, but we cannot escape where we come from.

"Go to Galilee, and there they will see me"—*Matthew 28:10*

This is the very first command of the risen Lord! Why would he send them back to Galilee? It's quite simple. Isn't it true that when you really want to know someone, you try to retrace their steps, go back to their childhood, to their place of origins and growing up? It seems that the more important and famous a person is, the more we want to know about their background, those little unsuspected aspects and even secrets that make them the unique person they are. No one ever writes a definitive biography of an individual. Every attempt will be only bits and pieces, and there will always be a bit more, another small but crucial detail that throws light on the whole. Even the best of biographies can only hope to approximate the mystery of the person they are writing about. This does not mean that biographies are not truthful or useful, but merely that there will always be more to say.

We are very much shaped by the many experiences of our formative years. The fears and prejudices, hurts and aspirations, dreams and vision, curses and blessings of the people we are raised among become part of our inner being and our ordinary language. The environment, the people, their social struggles, and everything about their home territory become part of the revelation into the ultimate identity and personality of the person. The more we can learn about a person's background, the more we can understand and appreciate who he or she truly is.

The Gospels, although not biographies in the modern sense of the word, nevertheless give us various aspects of the living memory of Jesus of Nazareth. They are not a fictional creation of someone's imagination. They are based on the memory of one who was born, raised, and lived among them, ate with them, taught them, was condemned to death, and was resurrected from the dead. They try not just to present what his life and message were but who he was in the context of his time and society. Who he was makes his life and message all the more startling—more fascinating and more generative of faith, courage, and hope. Because God became human in Jesus of Nazareth, every aspect of his earthly origins and identity will open up new areas of revelation into the mystery of our redemption (Catechism 515). His very being, coupled with his life, will be what he himself announced in the synagogue in Nazareth: sight to the blind, liberty to the captives, and freedom to the enslaved (Luke 4:18–19).

"God chose the foolish of the
world to shame the wise"—*1 Corinthians 1:27*

Often in working with the poor who have been imprisoned for petty mistakes or with those seeking to escape the daily torture of living in misery by getting into drugs, I have discovered that the Jesus of the Gospels becomes a real source of rebirth. Their insights into the gospel texts are astounding. I remember Jaime, a young ex-drug addict and ex-prisoner from one of the poor barrios in San Antonio who had discovered Jesus while in prison. He came from one of those areas of the world of which you could ask, "Can anything good come from there?" The poor areas of San Antonio were plagued with inadequate schools, no public libraries, overcrowded homes, and a level of poverty that resulted in malnutrition, poor hygienic conditions, and underemployment. The horrible conditions have led many of our young people into drugs just to escape the horrors and hopelessness of daily life.

From the lowest pits of human existence Jaime had risen to the highest peaks through his personal encounter with Jesus. His language was a rich barrio mixture of Spanish and English that would not be acceptable in any school or pulpit. His language was horrible to the linguistic purists, but the substance of his thought was astounding. He was the leader of my youth Bible group, which gathered about a hundred teenagers every Wednesday night to pray and listen to the Word of God. Jaime would explain the Scriptures to them in language none of us would dare to use in the pulpit or classroom, but a language which made the Jesus message come alive for the teenagers. He had only completed eighth grade and never studied Scriptures or much of anything else, yet his insights into the meaning of the text were fascinating. I was constantly amazed at his wisdom. Once I brought in a biblical scholar to listen to him. We both agreed that this young man truly had the grace of interpretation. He had no formal studies, but he expressed insights richer and far beyond many of those found in the finest of biblical commentaries.

In many ways, Jaime was like a modern Galilean Jesus. His own experience of deprivation, marginalization, and suffering gave him insights into the saving and liberating dynamics of Jesus that many of us had not suspected. He was considered nothing by the world. I am sure that because of his past record I would not have been able to get him into the seminary even if he had wanted to be a priest. Yet I am convinced he was anointed by God to bring young people to Christ. They flocked to him in great numbers, and some even claimed that they had been healed through his prayers. Was he performing miracles? For some, there was no doubt. Yet upon seeing and hearing Jaime, others wondered how I could allow such a "trashy" and "uncultivated" man to lead our youth prayer group and no doubt asked in their hearts: "Can anything good come from the barrios of the poor?"

"Can anything good come from Nazareth?"—*John 1:46*

When the apostle Philip approached Nathaniel with the exciting news that the long-awaited Messiah who had been spoken of by Moses and the prophets was among them, Nathaniel responded in utter dismay and disbelief: "Can anything good come from Nazareth?" (John 1:46). Galilee was a vast frontier region that had gone through various invasions and was presently a colony of Rome and under the influence of Greek culture. It was the crossroads to everywhere but the center of nowhere. It was not just the crossroads of travelers and caravans—it was the crossroads of civilizations. It was considered to be a land filled with the darkness of ignorance (Matthew 4:16) and the contamination brought about by the various peoples who lived there. What good could come from such a mess?

Galilee does not appear to have any special importance in the Old Testament, and it appears to have had a rather negative connotation even in the times of Jesus. Yet it is an all-important location in the life and ministry of Jesus. This is the place where his flesh and spirit took shape and would be his basic earthly identity and that of many of his earliest followers.

By living and growing up in Galilee, one came into contact with the various civilizations, cultures, and religions of the world. These exchanges would be very ordinary in Galilee but would be abhorred by any "purist" as evidence of decay and contamination. Like all peoples who live in the borderlands, the Galileans were looked down upon by those who lived in the great centers of civilization: the Jews who lived there were far away from the Temple, while the Greeks who lived there were far away from their athenaeum and gymnasiums. But this vast *frontera*, this land of darkness and confusion, was to become the light of the nations (Matthew 4:15) and the cradle of the new humanity inaugurated by Jesus.

It is Galilee that gave Jesus all his particularities: his language, his accent, his social status, his experience of mixing with different peoples, prejudices, purity codes, taboos, and other such identifying elements. It is precisely in the way that Jesus related to his multiethnic and multilingual society and its customs, reacted to them, offered a new vision together with new alternatives for daily living, and was even willing to die for the positions he took in relation to the structures and traditions of the times that the shackles of sin were broken and redemption took place.

At a time when racial purity was an obsession with many of the people, the Jews in Galilee were looked down upon. They were considered not only ignorant of the law but also impure because of their regular contacts with the gentiles who lived all around them (Freyne 1988, 216–217). The Messiah was not supposed to come from there! Knowing the natural tendencies and drives of human beings, I have no doubt that a very natural cultural, linguistic, and bodily *mestizaje* was taking place throughout Galilee. Yet mestizos are always looked upon as "unacceptable" by both parent groups. They are the most marginal of all peoples.

Yet it is in this place where the margins of various civilizations of the world intermingled, a place inhabited by many peoples of different ethnicities and religions and of no particular importance or renown, that the good news of a new creation would erupt. In a place where the various purity codes of humanity, which brand some as acceptable while marking others as impure and unacceptable, Jesus would assume religious-cultural impurity only to reveal the falsity of such codes and to introduce a totally new code of purity and belonging. It would not be based on any established code of exclusion, but simply on the acceptance of God's unmerited love that allows us to love ourselves and others as God loves us.

"The Messiah will not come from Galilee"—*John 7:41*

The God of the Bible is the God of incredible surprises. We would have expected the Savior of humanity to come from one of the great centers of the world. Some, because of the *Pax Romana*, which brought relative peace and prosperity to the world through the military force of Rome, thought that Caesar could well be the promised Messiah. Others might have thought that the new humanity of peace and prosperity would come through the rational philosophers of Greece. The Jewish people were expecting the Messiah to come from God as a triumphant military leader in the style of King David.

Today, like in times of old, we expect the world to be saved through military power and might. We spend incredible sums of money on instruments of war. We think that science, economic prosperity, and military might will bring about world peace. So we think of the great capitals of the world. These might help, but they will not bring it about.

Religious scholars of the dominant societies look to each other for the latest breakthroughs in religious thought that will bring light to the world, but they disregard or consider as unimportant the works coming out of the margins of the dominant world.

God chose not to come into the world through any of the great centers of power, knowledge, and influence. This is the foolishness and wisdom of God. Out of a region that had been marginal and dis-

tant from any of the various power games for control and domination—whether economic, social, intellectual, or religious—God
chose to have the savior of humanity emerge. He would not engage
in the various power games for control and domination. He would
not waste time with tenure games in the universities nor seek hierarchical climbing in religious institutions. He would not be guard-
ing his assets on Wall Street or pushing for a new position in the
corporation. Way out in the margins of all power structures, he
would be free to initiate something radically new and liberating for
everyone.

Why Galilee? Why *La Frontera*?

The first answer to the question "Why Galilee?" could be quite simple and totally correct: Because that is what God wanted! And who
am I to question the ways of God or to dare to assign reasons to the
actions of God? I am not God's counselor.

God has revealed his identity throughout time in many ways but
in a privileged way through the dynamics of revelation as manifested
through the Hebrew people, recorded in the Bible, and, in the fullness of time, through his Son who became human for our salvation.
In the struggles for freedom, identity, and land of the Hebrew people, God was acting and speaking on behalf of the poor and dispossessed of the world, who are often the victims of the greed of the
more powerful. Yet even the poor and the oppressed of this world
can become cruel, stubborn, and closed into themselves. Histori-
cally, human groups have evolved through their contacts with other
peoples. It is in the exchange that takes place between persons and
human groups that humanity advances. Yet colonized and dominated groups fear contact with dominant powers because they fear
that their ways will be destroyed and they will cease to exist—a type
of ethnocide.

In the life and teachings of Jesus, it is evident that Jesus identi-
fies himself with the outcasts and "public sinners" of society as he

offers them a new sense of dignity, identity, and belonging. Not only does Jesus enter into personal contact with the outcasts of his own people, but he dares to scandalize his people by entering into contact with foreigners such as the Samaritan woman, the Canaanite woman, and the Roman centurion. Through them, the nothings and undesired "others" of society, the world would begin to experience a new creation. So we could well say that God wants us to know the ways, the mind, and the heart of God—quite often in contrast to the ways of sinful humanity.

What has been very intriguing for me for a long time is that while God was revealing much through the history of the people of Israel, Galilee never played a significant part in the ongoing events. In fact, if anything, it appears to have a very negative role in that it was considered the Galilee of the gentiles, a land of undesirable and even despised ethnic mixture, a land of impurity both ethnic and religious. It was a marginal region of the world, and had it not been for Jesus, it would probably remain a relatively unknown and insignificant region of the world today.

As we penetrate into the mystery of the very dynamics of God's entry into the redemption of humanity, we must begin with the recognition that the biblical judgment is that humanity had sinned and gotten away from the ways of God. In its very efforts at empire-building, humanity was enslaving and crushing the weaker and more defenseless peoples of the world against the will and intention of the Creator. It wasn't human development itself that was sinful but the buildup of families and nations at the cost of enslaving and destroying other peoples. The great mystery of the ways of God is that God will not use the logic of power of this world but will instead introduce a new power, totally unsuspected by the powers of this world.

God chooses the Hebrew people to be his own. Who were they in relation to the world? They were the nobodies, the feared strangers and immigrants, the "other" unwanted by the landowners of the dominant societies. The very name "Hebrew" seems to come from an ancient word, 'apiru, meaning the peoples without a name or without an identity. It is these very peoples that are roaming around unprotected by any of the powerful deities of that time that God chooses for God's very own. It is to these people that God says: "I have witnessed the affliction of my people . . . and heard their cry . . . I know well what they are suffering . . . I have come down to rescue them"(Exodus 3:7–8). Thus begins the pattern of whom God chooses to bring about redemption: not the wise and powerful, not the wealthy and famous, not the dominant and well-installed but those deprived of their basic humanity by the unjust structures of this world. Those that the world considers insignificant and inferior God redeems by choosing them to be his very own—and God chooses only the best, never trash!

But they are chosen not to overthrow the powerful by their own ways and weapons but by ushering in new ways, values, and ideas so as to build a more human society for everyone. Out of their own suffering, they are called to create a society where no one will have to suffer. Their suffering is the basis of their call, not to canonize suffering as if it was something good in itself but to struggle to eliminate the very root causes of the suffering.

This pattern of choosing the rejected of this world to begin the new creation is consistent not only throughout the Hebrew Scriptures, but comes to a high point in Jesus the Galilean, Son of Mary, and continues today through the apparitions of Mary—to the Indian Juan Diego, the peasant girl Bernadette, and the peasant children of Fatima.

So in following this pattern, we continue to dig into the question, Why Galilee? Jesus was a marginal peasant from a marginal region of the world. Certainly he was a very extraordinary man, just like the Niño Fidencio in northern Mexico or Don Pedrito Jaramillo in Southern Texas or other local charismatic leaders and faith healers. In spite of their great abilities and great following, they were still marginal persons in every way in relation to the dominant society. This marginal identity certainly fits into the pattern of who God chooses.

But it seems to me there is more to the choice of Galilee. The great sin of the world is how people use the very beautiful uniqueness of ethnic and religious particularity to segregate people, separate them from each other, exclude the unwanted groups, exploit them, make some think of themselves as inferior, ugly, and unworthy, and even create violent animosities against each other. The powerful define the weaker as inferior and do not hesitate to enslave them. Isn't this the great sin of the world today? A few years ago we thought that the greatest threat to world peace was communism; today it is very clear that the greatest threat to world peace is ethnic-religious hatreds. These are the basis of our wars today. They could well be the basis of ethnic-religious gangs throughout the United States that could turn our neighborhoods into battlefields.

Jesus grew up, by God's design, in an unimportant region of the world where various peoples lived, worked, and entered into commerce together. This was not an ideological attempt to build a new multiethnic society where religious tolerance and interchange would thrive. It was simply the practical way of survival at the margins of the well-defined ethnic societies where the ordinary rules and taboos against ethnic mixture were not as rigidly enforced. In this marginal region of the world the boundaries that keep peoples apart were pretty well blurred, not out of principle but out of everyday practical needs.

Humanly speaking, Jesus grew up appreciating the positive value of the various peoples he encountered and even of the mixture and synthesis of ideas, traditions, and customs. While being a devout and loyal Jew, his childhood experience enabled him to appreciate the value and dignity of others, no matter how different they were. It also enabled him to relativize the borders of separation created by races, ethnicities, and religions by experiencing how one can be very loyal and faithful to one's own while appreciating and even being enriched by the "otherness" of the others. The differences in ethnicities and religions do not destroy us or make us impure. Quite the opposite, they enrich us and even make us more human. The stupidity and cruelty of segregation stands in stark contrast to the wisdom and beauty of friendships beyond any borders. God used Jesus' formative years in Galilee as the basis for initiating the new reign of God—a new family beyond the blood, social, ethnic, racial, or religious differences the world uses to separate and classify peoples.

Why Galilee? Precisely because of its ethnic mixture, it was a good place to begin the new universal fellowship that Jesus came to initiate. Because Galilee was a crossroads between the great humanly constructed civilizations and religions of the world, it was a great place for the reign of God as lived and proclaimed by Jesus to begin. From among the peoples who were considered the least by the greats of this world, the greatest of this world would emerge. Truly, as Paul brings out in the first epistle to the Corinthians: "God chose the foolish of the world to shame the wise, and God chose the weak of the world to shame the strong, and God chose the lowly and despised of the world, those who count for nothing, to reduce to nothing those who are something" (1 Corinthians 1:27–28).

This great crossroads of ancient civilizations, this frontier land that marked the outer limits of one and the beginning of another geo-ethnic religious region, would now become the cradle of the new humanity, a humanity open to all the ethnicities of the globe.

In one of the earliest texts of the first Christians we find another important clue to the redemptive meaning of the earthly social identity of Jesus: "He [Jesus] is the stone rejected by you the builders" (Acts 4:11). The earthly Jesus whose divinity was masked by the stereotypes of his sociocultural identity was the ultimate reject of his socially constructed world. He was the one no one would have chosen to play on their team, admitted into the prestigious schools of his time, welcomed into their clubs, or even allowed to enter a seminary in preparation for priestly formation. In fact, many of today's Christian churches would have probably not wanted him around, would not have allowed him into their congregations.

The builders of this sinful world, that is, the builders of the social, political, economic, and even religious empires of this world, would not have wanted him around—except as cheap labor to do the work no one else wanted to do. His social identity kept his true identity as an authentic human being from being recognized and accepted. This is not surprising since sin distorts our ability to see the truth, especially the truth of the human. No wonder his people were angered and scandalized when Pilate presented him to them as their king! And for Pilate it was the ultimate way of insulting the Jewish people: by presenting this marginal Galilean peasant as their leader. Sin destroys our ability to see and appreciate the truth, the goodness, and the beauty of the human: that every human being is created to the image and likeness of God and is invited to participate in the ongoing creation of the world God has entrusted to our care.

"The beginning of the gospel of Jesus Christ"—Mark 1:1

The earliest written memory of Jesus is the gospel according to Mark. He begins and ends the "good news" with stories of Galilee. As John remembers it in his gospel account, Jesus worked the first of his many signs and miracles in Cana in Galilee, and it was in Galilee that the apostles were called and where much of the activity of Jesus took place. After the resurrection, it was in Galilee that they would see him.

In becoming a Galilean, Jesus becomes an impure man, that is, impure according to the codes of purity of sinful humanity. Those who are outside these purity codes become the undesirables and untouchables of society. They are the victims of the sin of the world. In furthering the "emptying" of all social status, the Son of God takes on the flesh of "impure" humanity so as to enter into solidarity with those suffering with this stigma. But it is not just to suffer that he becomes a Galilean; he does so to destroy these external signs of purity and reveal the true purity: the purity of the clean heart. The builders of this world might think of development, renewal, and reform, but given the state of affairs of humanity, a totally new beginning was necessary.

At the core of Christian belief is the conviction that it was through the death and resurrection of Jesus that our salvation was achieved. Through him, wounded humanity was rehabilitated, healed, redeemed. What makes this all the more powerful and effective in the lives of ordinary people is the fact that it was Jesus, who came from Nazareth, a town in multiethnic Galilee, who was crucified, resurrected, and installed by God as the Lord of nations, judge of the living and the dead. It wasn't just any man who died for our sins, but the very specific individual named Jesus of Nazareth, the carpenter of Galilee of the pagans (Matthew 4:15), the son of Mary of Nazareth.

Grace works through nature, and God works through the events of human history. God used this crossroads of peoples and civilizations to begin the ultimate unity of all peoples, not a unity that would impose one civilization over the others but one that would combine elements of each one to form something truly new. No one would be destroyed, but all would be enriched by the others. No one people alone could save humanity, not even the chosen people of the Hebrew covenant. It would take elements of many to begin forming the mosaic of the new humanity that would truly reflect the image and likeness of God, the God who created all peoples to God's own image and likeness.

It is in Galilee that the body of the Word made flesh came to adult life, and it is through this Galilean body and spirit that the truth of the human and the truth of God will be revealed to humanity. This is truly one of the great mysteries of the mind and heart of God, not a mystery that cannot be solved but one which allows us to appreciate all the more the unsuspected magnanimity of God's love.

> Land of Zebulum and land of Naphtali,
> the way to the sea, beyond the Jordan,
> Galilee of the Gentiles,
> the people who sit in darkness
> have seen a great light,
> on those dwelling in a land overshadowed by death
> light has arisen.
>
> —Matthew 4:15–16

~

CHAPTER SIX

A Transformative Experience

**"He made him to be sin who
did not know sin"**—*2 Corinthians 5:21*

Jesus became like us in all things, except sin, yet he was made sin! What a startling statement. He was made to suffer the consequences of sin that he might eradicate sin at its deepest roots: "that we might become the righteousness of God in him" (2 Corinthians 5:21). Sin not only blinds us from seeing and appreciating the truth, especially the truth about human beings, it also perverts our way of seeing, understanding, and judging ourselves and others. The sin of the world is the great lies created by the powerful about their victims—that they are inferior, irresponsible, impure, immoral, and irresponsible—an ongoing litany of insulting and degrading notions. Thus innocent victims of injustice are easily regarded as ugly and inferior while the perpetrators of injustice appear as good, beautiful, holy, and the models of true human beings.

The great curse of the sin of the world is that, over time, many of the victims began to believe the falsehood created about them. Even if they do not believe what is said about them, they still suffer the consequences. The worst and most devastating form of enslavement

and spiritual imprisonment is when the victims began to believe all
the horrible things said about them by the dominant society, when
they began to think of themselves as unworthy, undignified, and impure. In the same way, when Jesus became sin, he did not sin personally, but he suffered the consequences of sin: he was misjudged,
maligned, ridiculed, and put down.

The distance between the real identity of Jesus and the identity
attributed to him by his society and contemporaries is astronomical.
Isn't this one of the great sources of suffering, anxiety, and even embarrassment in our own lives: the distance between what society and
family say that we are and what we know ourselves to be? The great
disaster is that often we begin to believe the bad things others think
of us. This is the dehumanizing and enslaving distance between
what Jesus really was and what people thought and said that he was.
He became one of those that sinful society labels falsely as illegitimate, impure, and inferior and finds ways of excluding from the various structures of society, especially from the parties and fiestas of
the "pure and beautiful" people of the dominant society. If they dare
challenge or get out of line, they are easily discredited or eliminated
altogether. Did Jesus begin to believe all the bad things people said
about him? No one will ever know, but it certainly must have hurt
even if he knew them to be false.

Jesus probably suffered many ugly slurs during his childhood, the
type of remarks that dig deep into the heart and consciousness of a
person and can damage the psyche for life. He was a marginal Jewish Galilean peasant and would probably speak with the speech pat-
terns of such a person and with a mixed language like our own
Tex-Mex. This alone would earn him the ridicule of the city
dwellers and more sophisticated society. But there was even more.
The issue of his real father and tales about the mysterious conception would abound easily in the small town of Nazareth, as they do
in any small town. I am sure that Mary was not considered "blessed"
by her own generation and townsfolk and that her son was not recognized as anything special by those around her. It is quite possible,

and I think even very probable, that even the immediate extended family of Jesus might make insulting remarks and jokes about him. Often, the most cruel insults and nicknames take place within the family and neighborhood. They are especially cruel and quickly spread in a small town where gossip, especially ugly rumors, is the main entertainment of the town. Even in his recorded lifetime, there are many indications of the many accusations he endured: born of fornication (John 8:41), possessed by a demon (Mark 3:22), crazy (Mark 3:21), rebel rouser, agitator, friend of outcasts, and even a glutton and a drunkard (Matthew 11:19, Luke 7:34).

The deepest and most devastating shame one has to live with is the existential awareness that because I am who I am, society and especially those in authority consider me to be illegitimate, inferior, and unwanted; good enough for the work no one else wants to do, but never good enough to fully belong to the mainstream and dominant group. No matter how much I improve myself and manage to work myself into the structures of the mainstream, remarks and innuendos will remind me that I am not fully one of them. Children of racial minorities grow up seeing themselves as stained and ugly. Children of marginal minorities, especially racial minorities, grow up with this dehumanizing stigma. Mestizo children grow up with the double stigma of not being fully accepted by either of the parent groups. This becomes all the more painful and complicated when the father refuses to acknowledge, claim, and name the child. Even society gives a horrible name to children born out of wedlock, and when anyone does something horrible, he or she is referred to by that name: bastard. Existential shame is very profound and one of the most painful aspects of life one has to live with.

Jesus was constantly accused of various wrongdoings and eventually even condemned to death. He defended himself but never sought to get revenge. Jesus was not into revenge, but into forgiveness, a forgiveness that rehabilitated both the offender and the offended into their original innocence. Even when they subjected him to the most horrible violence possible, he continued his life-giving and liberating practice of forgiveness. This is the only way to healing, inner freedom of the spirit, and peace. Revenge only results in self-destruction.

How could any human person who grew up as Jesus did be as self-assured, understanding, compassionate, and forgiving as Jesus? Throughout his life he was victimized often and in many ways. I am sure the worst insults were not even recorded in our Scriptures, but in his public life he never gives into self-pity, revenge, or the need to punish the victimizers. He would not become a victim turned victimizer! What enabled Jesus to endure the injustices and social insults yet not give in to the spirit of shame, guilt, or revenge? It would be a denial of his humanity if we thought that he did not feel any pain, disgust, or even anger. There are clear indications when his anger led him to prophetic and heroic proclamations and actions. What enabled him to go through the pain and anger that often destroys people into something totally new and wonderful, into a new appreciation of true purity, a new basis of ultimate identity and into a new source of belonging? What enabled this man of suffering to turn into the great visionary and prophet of love?

No one ever knows what really goes on in the minds and hearts of other persons, and we will never know what was going on in the life of Jesus before the beginning of his public ministry. But knowing what goes on in the lives of racial minorities living in the small towns of Texas, we can well suspect what went on in the life of the marginal Jewish peasant from Galilee. As much as he loved his family and cultural traditions, he must have felt equally, as many of our young people do today, totally corralled and suffocated by them. He needed to get out of there or he would become a zombie!

"From that time on, Jesus began to preach"—*Matthew 4:17*

Jesus leaves his work, his town, and his family and goes not to the cultural-religious center of his people in Jerusalem but to the desert to see John the Baptist, who was proclaiming a simple but revolutionary message: Repent, for the kingdom of heaven is at hand (Matthew 3:34)! His message is simple and to the point. It was easy for the masses to grasp. No complicated dogmas or rituals. The masses, the *massa damnata*, often oppressed by the guilt imposed by their own religious leaders, flock to him. Jesus is at home with this searching mob; he is one of them, and they are his own people, the marginal and often despised people of society who think of themselves as inferior and unworthy.

John calls for a repentance, for the kingdom of God is near. Repent not just from the bad things you have done, but most of all from not trusting sufficiently in the goodness and loving providence of God. Repent from your way of thinking, from believing all the lies the Temple priests, Pharisees, Sadducees, and others are saying about your uncleanness and unworthiness. Repent from the greatest injustice of all: not believing in yourself, believing that God made you inferior to others and less dignified than them. The repentance calls for a change of attitude about oneself and others, for in the kingdom of God all will enjoy the radical equality of being children of a loving and caring God. Going into the water is a burial of the past, of past attitudes and hurts, of old ways of thinking about oneself and others. Going into the water is a drowning of the false, dehumanizing, and paralyzing identities imposed by sinful structures, while the coming out is the emergence of a person cleansed of the feelings and attitudes of uncleanness, unworthiness, and inferiority. Coming out of the water is the beginning of a radical change in life. Jesus, too, undergoes this change: from his quiet life in Nazareth to a provocative pubic life, from the typical resignation of the poor, "*pues así es la vida*" ("well, such is life"), to a dynamic activism in favor of a new life. The victim of sin becomes not the avenger but the artisan of life.

Jesus' coming to join the masses seeking new life and his baptism by John was a profound religious experience that the early Christian community could not forget or ignore. This event marked a great change in the life of Jesus: from his hidden life in Nazareth to his active life of preaching, healing, forgiving, and feasting till the end of his life. Jesus experienced divine love and became the agent of this love, making it available to everyone. "From that time on, Jesus began to preach" (Matthew 4:17). In *Cursillos* and other pastoral moments, I have witnessed how a particular religious experience can totally change the life of a person, heal them of past hurts, and fill them with a new spirit. Quiet, fearful, bashful persons have been converted into articulate, fearless apostles. We don't know what happened before in Nazareth, but we do know that from this moment on, Jesus appears publicly as a self-assured, daring, and articulate artisan of the new life of love. This was a love that would challenge all humanly made barriers that kept people from loving God, themselves, and others. What brought about the change from a silent and hidden life to a very public and articulate one?

"You are my beloved son; with you I am well pleased"—*Luke 3:22*

From the beginning of his public life it is clear that Jesus experienced a tremendous sense of God's approval and unquestioned love: "You are my beloved Son; with you I am well pleased" (Luke 3:22). It is this intimate love that gave Jesus the power to feel pain, sadness, and even anger and not be consumed by them. It was a love that was frequently nurtured through intimate conversation with the one who truly understands and knows: our loving and caring *Abba*. The experience of being loved unconditionally by a meaningful person is a great source of healing and strength. The more we are loved, the more we can love. Yet the best of human love will always be limited in many ways and can easily end in tragedy. Just look at the tragic love turned to hate that is evidenced in so many divorce cases.

There is only one love that will never betray us, that will never abandon us, that will always be there to accompany us and strengthen us on the way. Only the experience of God's love can enable us to love as God loves: without limit! This is the love that enabled Jesus to rise above the insults and injuries of others and to respond not with counterinsults and injuries but with the overpowering power of love. It was the personal experience of this divine love that put all of life into a new perspective, for nothing is more liberating and life giving than the experience of being loved. What do the crazy and malicious judgments of the world matter when I know I am accepted, valued, and loved by the one who is above all else, by the one who truly knows it all, by the one who is the author and ultimate judge of life?

I came to a deep appreciation of what Jesus' awareness of God as his loving and intimate father could mean to a person through one of my parishioners. Joe was a very attractive young man who had another job during the day but liked to walk the streets at night looking for older men. Occasionally he would drop by the church to light a candle. Gradually we became friends, and one day he told me his story. He was the son of a mistress and a father who would not recognize him as his son. He knew who his father was, but his father would not recognize him as his son.

He had only made physical contact with his father twice in his life. Once when he was a young child, the father had spent the night with his mother, and while the father was drinking his morning coffee, Joe playfully had hit the cup and spilled it over his lap. The man became so angered and violent that he slapped the boy so hard that he burst his eardrum, leaving Joe deaf in one ear.

A few years later, the man's legitimate son started making fun of Joe in the school playground for being a bastard son. Joe became angry and got into a big fight with his half-brother. That night, the father came to Joe's house to give him a whipping for daring to insult his real son. He gave him such a strapping that for several days it was hard for him to sit down.

Why was Joe walking the streets looking for older men? As he told me, he liked women, but at nights he felt he was searching for the embrace of the father, the embrace he had never received from his father. He had seen other fathers playing with their children, hugging and kissing them. He had really wanted this, but he had never had it. The only thing he really wanted in life was to some-day have his father recognize him, put his arm around him, and sim-ply call him "my son." He wasn't asking for anything else, but the basic recognition that he was his son.

Knowing who his father was and longing for the recognition of being his son was a painful wound and caused a deep loneliness that he tried to heal and compensate for in the streets of San Antonio. He told me he really didn't enjoy the sex, but he loved the embrace and the caresses he would receive from the older men whose ad-vances he would accept. He would sort of brag: "I'm pretty picky; I turn down most of the advances. I can tell a weirdo a mile away."

I didn't want to scare him away by preaching to him too quickly. Gradually I told him how Jesus might have gone through something similar, since people did not know who his earthly father was, and I was sure there must have been plenty of rumors. He was fascinated by this. As the conversations continued, we gradually started to talk about Jesus' fascination with God as "Abba," as *Papacito*, as "Daddy." God is the ultimate Father of all of us, and even the ones who do not have an earthly father to recognize them as their children still have God as the loving Father who calls them by name, embraces them, and says, "This is my beloved child."

Joe enrolled in our "Rite of Christian Initiation for Adults (RCIA) for quick learners" and in going through the program expe-rienced a rebirth; it was a real resurrection experience. He found in-credible healing and liberation in saying the "Our Father" and one day he told me: "It really feels good to call you father." I don't think I have ever received a more beautiful compliment. But even better yet was his simple confessional statement one day. In a somewhat laughing way, he stated: "I'm sleeping better these days; I don't have to walk the streets at night anymore."

He cried great tears of joy the night of his baptism; for him it was a real death, a thorough cleansing and purification of his previous life. He joined the choir, became active in the parish, found a beau-tiful girlfriend, and today is happily married and very dedicated to his children. "I never want my children to suffer what I have suffered."

I never asked him to stop his streetwalking. By simply walking with him through his life, never condemning but only seeking to understand with the compassion of Jesus, gradually inviting him into alternatives he had not suspected even existed, he found a new life! Incredible as it sounds to many, the simple but profound recognition that God is our Father, my Father who loves me beyond what any human father could love, was the "good news" which he had never known and that brought redemption to him.

"Glad tidings to the poor"—*Luke 4:18*

Jesus comes out of this transformative experience to offer it to others. The intimate and empowering love of God that Jesus experienced was not just for himself alone, but for everyone else as well. The very personal experience of the absolute gratuitous love of God would transform people. It would be the basis of the new life; it would be the basis of new insights; it would form new criteria of judgment; and it would be a force that would enable people to walk and act in radically new ways: "The Spirit of the Lord is upon me, because he has anointed me to bring glad tidings to the poor. He has sent me to proclaim liberty to captives and recovery of sight to the blind, to let the oppressed go free, and to proclaim a year acceptable to the Lord" (Luke 4:18–19).

Jesus did not come just to make the poor feel good about themselves so that they might remain in the misery of poverty. He wants much more than for the poor to live on handouts or welfare. Reaching out to those in need is definitely the criteria of the fullness of our humanity and the sign that people can be counted among the "saved"—it is not good works that earn us salvation, but our good works are the product of a redeemed life, of the life of grace. In order to develop the privilege of reaching out to those in need, of having something to offer others, we must develop the talents and gifts God has given each one of us. Extreme poverty and misery, prolonged oppression and marginalization, often keep people from even being aware they have possibilities to develop! Jesus calls us to the fullness of life, to the fullness of our potential, to the fullness of our development so that we might be able to help others who are still on the way or have not even had the opportunity of beginning. Jesus begins by opening the eyes of people so that they may see themselves and society as they truly are.

I remember a lady from one of the very poor barrios of San Antonio. During one of our Bible study sessions, she stated: "I love to study the Gospels because I often discover good things about myself I had never suspected. It feels so great that I can't wait to leave and put them into practice." Indeed, she was experiencing the good news of Jesus.

Jesus came that the poor might hear the good news (Luke 4:18) that they are not trash or inferior but lovely and lovable children of the same God as everyone else. He came that the lame might walk— that those that had been paralyzed by society's subjection and lamed by society might jump and leap into new opportunities. He came that the blind might see—that people could open their eyes and see with the eyes of God, see creation and especially see human beings as God sees and values them, that those blinded by the labels placed upon them might see their many talents and capabilities and begin to develop them (Matthew 11:15, 15:30; Luke 7:22). He came that the captives might be liberated—that people might be liberated from the incarceration of their own low self-esteem, lack of self-confidence, and most of all futility and begin to believe in themselves. He came that the oppressed might go free—that those enslaved by the unjust structures of this world might break the shackles of oppression and begin a new creation where no one will be oppressed again. They would be free not to oppress others as others had oppressed them, but to do good for others as God has done for us. The measure of true freedom is our ability to do good for others! Truly, for freedom he assumed our condition and gave his life for us: "For you were called for freedom, brothers. But do not use this freedom as an opportunity for the flesh; rather, serve one another through love" (Galatians 5:13). Christ won the freedom for us to become the artisans and builders of

a new creation, the responsible and creative artisans of our own society and civic world.

"Who are my mother and [my] brothers?"—Mark 3:33

The new appreciation of God, self, and others will very naturally
produce a new family—not of blood but of the spirit. No one is
without parents, for God is the loving parent of everyone. No one
need be without loving brothers and sisters, because there is now a
greater and more lasting family into which everyone is invited.

Precisely because of the hurts and pains of his past, Jesus can understand the suffering of those who were living in similar situations,
and he will go out of his way to bring them into the new community
of love and fellowship: "But he said to them in reply, 'Who are my
mother and [my] brothers?' And looking around at those seated in
the circle he said, 'Here are my mother and my brothers. [For] whoever does the will of God is my brother and sister and mother'"
(Mark 3:33–34). The real family is not the blood or ethnic family,
but all who are willing to put aside the old life and enter into the new
fellowship of love. It does not matter who your parents are, what your
family name is, where you are from, or what you have done in the
past; all that is quite irrelevant. What matters is your willingness to
die to the old categories of judgment and begin a new life of love.

The outcasts, the legally impure, the public sinners, the children,
the single women without a patriarch to protect them, the prostitutes, the destitute, and all those excluded from the Israelite community of holiness will be welcomed by Jesus; and furthermore it will
be through them that the long awaited kingdom of God will irrupt.
The radical acceptance and welcome of even the most destitute and
unwanted will be the basis of the new holiness community of Jesus
(Catechism 827). The others too will be welcomed, but most probably will not want to join with the very outcasts of their own society.

We cannot undo the past, but through the experience of God's intimate love and cleansing forgiveness we can retrieve it in such a way

as to allow it to become the energy of new life. The past does not disappear but is transcended. It is in this experience that the masks created by the identity attributed to us by society are dissolved and our real identity is revealed both to ourselves and to others. We are neither trash nor inferior but the beloved children of the loving God. It is in taking on the mind and heart of Jesus that our true self begins to flourish and a new life begins to flow from our newly discovered identity. We are not what the world says that we are, but what God knows us to be.

Having experienced the transforming power of God's love, we go into the waters of baptism to drown the old "inferior and undignified" self so as to come out of the water as a new person alive with energetic self-confidence, a liberated mind, and a loving heart (Catechism 1265). Indeed, the beginning of a new creation.

CHAPTER SEVEN

~

Restored Innocence

"Neither do I condemn you. Go, and from now on do not sin any more"—*John 8:11*

Guilt and resentment are two of the most aggressive cancers of the soul and probably a great factor in the various diseases of the body. They are destructive forces that transform friends and family into deathly enemies. They poison the heart, pervert the mind, and make life miserable for everyone. There seems to be a feeling that only through revenge and vengeance can rehabilitation take place. How wrong this is: The past can never be undone, but new life can arise out of it as the phoenix arises out of the ashes of the past. This is one of the great miracles of God's unlimited love. Through God's redeeming love, even the faults of the past can become the fuel of the new fire of love and the ingredients of the foods for the banquet table.

My good friend and colleague Daniel Groody tells of a powerful experience. "Many years ago while I was studying theology, I lived in a very comfortable house in Berkeley, California. I read about how God has a special love for the poor and the Church is called to make a preferential option for the poor. I struggled over the years to know exactly what that meant. This led me to spend some time simply interviewing people who were poor and underprivileged. I did not go out to prove anything, other than to listen to their stories. So I sat down on sidewalks next to beggars, homeless people, prostitutes, and other people who live on the streets. Their comments were very revealing.

"One of the most moving stories I had was when I went to Grand Central Station in New York City. I had some time to spare, so I went around talking to a few people, most notably prostitutes and bag ladies. On one occasion, there was a bag lady slumped over on the floor of Grand Central Station. Thousands of people walked by her and didn't even notice her. Her hair was a stringy gray, and she was dressed in a shabby, nylon coat. She was alone, very alone. So I went over to the coffee stand, bought two cups of coffee, and sat beside her. I gave her a cup of coffee and asked, 'How are you doing,' and she said, abruptly and curtly, 'Fine.' 'What's new?' 'Nothing,' she said with the same curt suspicion. 'How has your day been?' 'Good,' she murmured. Nothing. I realized I wasn't going to get very far. So I simply sat there and drank my coffee. There was a long pause from that moment on. And I just sat there and waited, determined to wait even if she never said another word. About twenty minutes later, she looked over at me, rather perplexed, and said, 'Who are you, anyway?' In no uncertain terms she wondered what the hell I was doing there, as just about everybody else had ignored her. Being nobody to anybody was a way of life for her. After her words broke our silence, I said to her, 'I am a priest.' To my surprise, those four words of mine broke her open on the inside. She began crying profusely, in loud, sobbing tears. I didn't know what to say, and I didn't want words to interfere. So I just sat with her in silence. It was a sacred kind of silence, one that I did not want to touch with words. It was more a moment to contemplate than complicate. But then after a long while, her tears subsided, allowing me to speak to her again. So I said, 'What is your name?' And she said, 'Sarah.' I said, 'Sarah, if you had the opportunity to change one thing in the world today, what would it be?' Thinking she would change the president, her homeless condition, or other structural evils in the world, she looked up at me and said, 'If I could change anything in the world today, I would change . . . my mind.' Stunned by her response, she taught me something important. She revealed something true about the human experience that I only faintly knew—the devastating pain of unhealed memories."

Whatever the hurts of this woman, whether she had been hurt by others or whether she had hurt others and was living in the pain and shame of guilt, she expressed the profound yearning of the mind and heart for cleansing. What she wanted the most was to let go of all the ugly and destructive thoughts that were tormenting her. Is this possible? Is it possible to be cleansed so completely that one begins to rejoice in the newly acquired innocence?

Our Nahuatl ancestors had the custom of having a priest come to a dying person so that in hearing the person's confession, the priest would absorb all the inner filth from the dying person, like an ink blotter absorbing the spilled ink. Hence the person would be thoroughly cleansed as he or she entered the journey into the other levels of life. Other religions have different ways of offering cleansing. The desire for cleansing is so deeply ingrained in our hearts that it can be found expressed in various ways in the different religious traditions of humanity.

Jesus did not want us to wait till the moment of death to began our cleansing. His invitation to repentance from the very beginning of his public ministry was an invitation to put on a new mind and heart: the mind and heart of God, who is a loving and merciful parent to all of us. Are we capable of accepting this love of God, which begins by a forgiveness which totally cleanses us so as to begin living a new innocence (Catechism 978)?

The notion of innocence calls forth many beautiful thoughts—purity of mind, of heart, of thoughts, of desires, of actions, of being. It brings forth notions of peacefulness, harmony, and spontaneity.

Innocence indicates freedom from any wrongdoing. When one has been accused of a crime, there are no more beautiful and rehabilitating words than the pronouncement by the jury of one's peers of "not guilty!" Our country's legal code is based on the presumption that one is innocent until proven guilty. Yet the mere accusation, even when one is innocent, is very damaging to the person.

One of the most beautiful aspects of Jesus' character was his innocence. Not an innocence of ignorance, but the beautiful innocence of one that is totally free of resentment or guilt. It is this innocence that Jesus invites us to rejoice in as we experience the undeserved, unlimited, and merciful forgiveness of our God who loves us beyond our wildest dreams. The experience of this forgiveness enables us to do what God alone can do: love ourselves and love others so much that we forgive those who have offended us and, even more so, accept forgiveness for the faults we have committed. Not because there is no shame, pain, or hurt, but because we now share in a love that surpasses all wrongdoing. Only love can triumph over the various currents of destructive evil active in humanity. This is the beginning of the new creation, the first step in a new journey of life.

The beauty of an innocent person, one truly free of any wrongdoing, deceit, or crime is astounding. It is unfortunate that we tend to equate innocence with ignorance or even with someone who is easily fooled or deceived. True innocence is neither ignorance nor naiveté but rather a state of purity of mind and heart. "Blessed are the clean of heart" (Matthew 5:8) could easily be translated as "Blessed are the innocent, the ones who do not offend anyone or harbor evil thoughts about self or others." Yet in the ordinary course of life, we will offend others and be offended by others. The offenses might be malicious or not even intended or suspected, but they still hurt and can still destroy us. Given this reality, the offer of Jesus for complete cleansing, for a complete restoration of one's inner health is indeed good news! It is the most beautiful possible healing of the wounded heart.

"This son of mine was dead,
and has come to life again"—*Luke 15:24*

One of the stories of Jesus that has inspired great art is the return of the prodigal son and his joyful reception by his Father (Luke 15:11–32). I suspect that it is because of our own feelings of shame and unworthiness and even of failure; the story reflects our own inner yearning to be fully and lovingly accepted by those who are especially meaningful to us and most of all by our God. The heart longs for the original innocence that we seemed to have lost somewhere along the journey of life and think that it is impossible to regain.

In the following moving story, Jesus once again surprises everyone by one of his typical reversals. It is the story of two brothers, but in a deeper sense it is the story of the two sides of many of us. In the deepest sense, in the merciful father, we see the story of every Christian who has truly put on the mind and heart of Christ to be merciful as the Father is merciful (Luke 6:36).

I think there is a bit of the prodigal son in each one of us; there is probably even more of the older brother; and unfortunately there is still way too little of the merciful father in us. As in the older brother of the story, our disgust with the mercy of God in relation to acknowledged sinners is often stronger than our sense of mercy and rejoicing at their comeback.

The younger brother is the side of us that lives in deep shame, remorse, and sorrow for things we have done in life that have offended others, especially those that we love the most, and that have disgraced us in the eyes of those who know us. If only we could undo the things we have done; if only we could undo the past. We long for that peacefulness and harmony before our offense ruptured or damaged the relationship. The stories of Jesus are so profound in their simplicity. What the younger son, the person who had strayed away from the goodness of the family home, missed the most was not the luxuries of life or even his old friends, but the taste of home cooking and the fellowship of the family table (Luke 15:17). Isn't it true that when we are away, even for a good purpose, it's the family cooking and fellowship that we miss the most? Thus the great feast with the abundance of the best of home cooking is the powerful sign that the sinful and arrogant young man of the past had been totally rehabilitated, totally cleansed, and totally integrated into the family. At the very core of our acceptance of God's unconditional forgiveness is the joyful participation in the festive meal of God's family, a family that excludes no one. (There is more on this in the next chapter; for now, it is sufficient to point to the connection between forgiveness accepted and the inclusive festive meal.)

I am sure that it is not surprising to any of us that when we hear this reading, we tend to feel sorry for the older brother and maybe even wonder if the father was not too soft on the younger one and too harsh on the older one. I know many family histories in which this has been the perceived case, and they have led to disaster. Does the story ridicule our efforts to live rightly and work hard at our duties? Not at all. After all, the struggle to be good and do the right things is a great task, and parents should recognize and reward these efforts and accomplishments. The older brother is the side of us that becomes proud of our own accomplishments, hardened by our own righteousness, and intolerant of the mistakes and weakness of others. Even more so, we become so focused on our efforts to do the right things and to appear upright in the eyes of others that we become oblivious to our own faults and mistakes. The pride and arrogance of the righteous often overshadow their goodness and sincerity. Their self-confidence overrides their confidence in God. Although it is a virtue to struggle to do the right things in life, the tragedy of the "righteous" is that often we become so focused on our own efforts that we fail to recognize and appreciate the grace of God at work in us. Unfortunately, the self-righteous often rejoice more in the condemnation of a sinner than in their rehabilitation. I often fear that our country is much more in this mind-set than into the merciful heart of God.

The sinner in us is convinced that our sin is so great that not even God can forgive us, while the righteous in us does not even think that we need God's forgiveness.

But there is even more in this story of Jesus. The father of the household breaks all the codes of honor and shame of his time by running to meet the returning son. Imagine an old patriarch having to pull up his robes, with probably weak knees, running through the village to welcome his returning son. You can imagine the laughter of the people as they watch this ridiculous spectacle. The wayward son is walking slowly toward the family home, but the father runs to greet the son. The father makes a fool of himself so as to absorb, like the Nahuatl ink blotter, the foolishness of the son. Rather than the people poking fun at the arrogant son who is now returning in failure and misery, they laugh at the foolishness of the old man and do not even notice the returning fool! This is the extent of the love of God for us. God makes a fool of himself so that our foolishness might fade into oblivion; God absorbs our filth so that we might be made clean!

The point of the story, central to the journey of salvation of Jesus in the gospel according to Luke, is not that the father is soft on one but harsh on the other. It is not as if God rewards waywardness and punishes goodness. This would be a pretty perverted God. The point of the story is precisely the unsuspected abundance of God's mercy in the context of the mystery of our human frailty. The story puts us right in the arena of ordinary human behavior. In the mystery of creation, we are all weak and in the course of time, mistakes will be made. "If we say, 'We have not sinned,' we make him a liar, and his word is not in us" (1 John 1:10).

It is amazing how we can bond so deeply with a person who has made similar mistakes as to those we have, and their recovery is a source of strength to us who are still in the pits. I once dealt with a young man who was attempting suicide. I tried all my best counseling and prayer techniques, but nothing worked. It was only when I started to share my own weakness with him and told him how, in a given crisis in my own life, I had gone for counseling to help me sort things out that he started to listen to me for the first time. He became fascinated with the idea that I, who seemed to be so sure of myself and secure, had also had to deal with human problems. From then on, he started to ask questions about how he could be helped. We got him to counseling, and he recovered beautifully. It was through my weakness that the grace of God came to him. I have often been reminded of Paul's words: "but he [Christ] said to me, 'My grace is sufficient for you, for power is made perfect in weakness.' I will rather boast most gladly of my weaknesses, in order that the power of Christ may dwell with me" (2 Corinthians 12:9). I sometimes wonder how our CV would look if we listed not only our successes but our mistakes, not only our strengths but also our frailties.

Thus in recognizing our weaknesses, we bond with the rest of humanity. Yet in our weakness, the very God who created us loves us even more, so as to convert our recognized and forgiven faults into the living cells of a new creation of love and generosity. Weakness is not converted into strength through discipline and duty but through the experience of unconditional acceptance and love. This is the great miracle of the story and of our personal stories as we grow in the experience of God's love.

"Not seven times, but seventy-seven times"—*Matthew 18:22*

The Gospels are full of incidents and teachings of Jesus where forgiveness is at the basis of the new life offered to us by him. It was such a reversal to the ordinary way of thinking, which saw forgiveness as a weakness and a sign of cowardice. It was even a greater reversal to that mind-set that feels that only through revenge or punishment of the offender can the offended obtain peace. Yet forgiveness is at the very core of repentance. We must repent not just from one action or another, or even from one bad habit or another, but from our ways of thinking and feeling so that we might put on the mind and heart of God, which is best expressed in the parable of the prodigal son and the merciful father. We must repent from the very mentality that demands revenge and restitution. Jesus reveals to us how forgiveness is the most powerful path to health, peace, freedom, tranquillity, and communitarian joy.

Forgiveness was definitely within the Jewish tradition of Jesus, but many conditions had to be fulfilled before forgiveness could be granted. In many ways, the offended seems to be the ultimate judge of whether forgiveness was deserved or not. This could easily lead to a form of revenge and righteous punishment. Jesus goes much further by placing the root of forgiveness not in the one offended, but in the very heart of God, our merciful parent.

Thus Jesus can tell the person caught in the very act of sin: "Neither do I condemn you. Go, and from now on do not sin any more" (John 8:11). When asked how often we have to forgive, he answers with a phrase meant to indicate infinity: "Not seven times, but seventy-seven times" (Matthew 18:22). When a sick person was brought to him, he healed him by forgiving his sins (Matthew 9:2–6). He taught about the justification of the sinner and the condemnation of the righteous (Luke 18:9–14). When the sinful woman washed his feet and the righteous were scandalized, in the original version of the New American Bible, Jesus stated "her sins, which are many, are forgiven, for she loved much" (Luke 7:47). In the beautiful prayer he gave us, we pray: "forgive us our sins for we ourselves forgive everyone in debt to us" (Matthew 6:9–13, Luke 11:2–4). When he was hanging from the cross in the agonizing moments before his death, he offered forgiveness to the very ones who condemned him: "Father, forgive them, they know not what they do" (Luke 23:34).

The very first action of the resurrected Lord, in keeping with the very core of his offer of new life, was to go to his very friends who had run out on him and offer them complete forgiveness. They had betrayed him; he offered them peace! His love for them was so great that even when they abandoned him in the hour of greatest need, he did not stop loving them. He did not go to demand explanations or apologies, but to offer them "peace," which is the consequence of forgiveness. All sense of guilt was gone and the joy of innocence ir-rupted. Yet his pain had not disappeared, for he showed them the wounds of his body and even asked them to touch them. Forgive-ness does not mean forgetting; for if you can forget you no longer have to forgive. Yet the very wounds are now the doorway to the new life. Jesus did not just return to the previous life, but he initi-ated a new life, not just for himself but for all of us.

"There will be rejoicing among the angels of God over one sinner who repents"—Luke 15:10

"Neither do I condemn you. Go, and from now on do not sin any more" (John 8:11). These are truly beautiful words to any one of us who has sinned or been accused of wrongdoing, rightly or wrongly!

Can any of us forget September 11 and its consequences? Can the Jews forget the Holocaust? Can the Japanese forget Nagasaki and Hiroshima? Can the prisoners of war forget the German, Japanese, or Viet Cong concentration camps? Can native Americans forget the European invasion, conquest, genocide, and domination? Can black Americans forget the brutality of their enslavement? Can a child forget the beatings of the alcoholic parent? Can a student for-get the unjust put-downs of a teacher? Can a friend forget the be-trayal of a friend?

The list could go on without end. Memories keep pain alive, and even when one tries to forget, it is impossible. The deeper the hurt, the greater the controlling influences of the aftermath. Depression, anxiety, feelings of anger mixed with feelings of unworthiness and inferiority become such a driving force in my daily life that "What I do, I do not understand. For I do not do what I want, but I do what I hate" (Romans 7:15).

I don't know of anything more horrible and destructive than hav-ing to live with the guilt and shame of having done something ugly and horrible. This is especially true if you have hurt someone you love very much. The greater the love, the deeper the pain of having hurt a loved one. If only the hurt could be undone. Our heart hungers for that innocence of our youth before we were conscious of having done anything wrong. Yet in this life, as we grow older, we become more and more aware and deeply ashamed of the mistakes that have marred our lives and, worst of all, the lives of others. We try to understand why we did whatever we did; we go to counselors and psychologists to help us understand, but understanding does not remove the guilt! Is there any way of recapturing the innocence of my youth?

Yet as I reflect upon this, there is something that is uglier and even more destructive, and that is to live with hate and disgust toward others who have offended me. In our perverted way of thinking, we feel that the only way we can be healed is by exerting some kind of punishment: "Make them pay!" But because "revenge" is not politically correct in our Christian vocabulary, we disguise our feelings by calling it justice. Revenge disguised as justice appears to be the best way to square off with those who have offended me. In fact, in this mentality, forgiveness appears not as a virtue, but as weakness. You only forgive when you are not strong enough to avenge yourself. And thus the cycle of evil continues to escalate, and one never arrives at either interior or exterior peace.

Jesus came to heal the wounds of humanity by reversing the powers of evil present in the world. There is no more personally devastating power than the spirit of shame and guilt and even more so the spirit of revenge. It not only destroys the enemy, it destroys the peace and tranquillity of the avenger. As long as there is hatred or guilt in our hearts, we cannot live in peace and harmony with ourselves or with others. Those who hate are totally dominated and controlled by the one they hate. They are not free to act but only react, and the hatred continues to poison much of their lives. Yet those who live in guilt cannot come to inner healing until they have experienced forgiveness; and those who live in shame of past actions cannot obtain peace until there is an experience of restored innocence. Forgiveness does not mean that the hurt is gone or that the wounds have disappeared; but it does mean that one rises above them to a new state of life and even to a new and more glorious state of life. The risen Lord took the initiative of going to the friends who had abandoned him in his hour of greatest need, not to scold them but to offer them peace. Yet he showed them his wounds and even asked them to touch them. The wounds were still there, but they no longer dominated or controlled his life.

To believe in Jesus is the beginning of our rebirth unto new life, of our experience of a new innocence. Through my faith in him I am liberated from the ordinary death traps of life. The more I believe in Jesus, the more his very life becomes my own life: "Yet I live, no longer I, but Christ lives in me" (Galatians 2:20). It is the Spirit of Christ alive in us that crushes our sinful inclinations to revenge and vengeance (Romans 8). It is likewise this Spirit that wipes out our shame. It is this Spirit that brings about, not just an adjustment in the self, but a total rebirth unto new life. It is this new life that empowers us to go beyond our ordinary inclinations, to reverse former values, and to live and act as Jesus did.

One of the most fascinating and liberating reversals introduced and practiced by Jesus was that of forgiveness. Only through forgiveness of self and of others can the heart be healed and the spirit be liberated for greater things. For Jesus and his followers, forgiveness was not a sign of weakness but rather a sign of the divine life that they had received. Forgiveness is love surpassing righteousness and divine mercy transcending human justice. Forgiveness is not a consequence of justice, but an outflow of divine generosity toward us which is now alive in us. If God forgives, who am I, sinner that I am, to condemn others? The sure sign that I have accepted God's forgiveness is that I will forgive others, and only in forgiving others can I myself be forgiven.

Forgiveness is not the last word but rather the first word of a new adventure, of a new partnership with the forgiving God and through this with all the community of forgiving brothers and sisters. The acceptance and offer of forgiveness are the beginning of a new fellowship of love and concern that will best be expressed, realized, and nourished through the joy of table fellowship. It is through forgiveness offered and received that we regain the innocence to enjoy the true freedom of the children of God. It is through forgiveness that animosity will be transformed into fellowship, strife into cooperation, and hatred into love. It is the only way to a true and lasting peace—among persons as among nations!

Blessed are the peacemakers, for they will be called children of God

—Matthew 5:9

CHAPTER EIGHT

~

Scandalous Fiestas

**"Why do you eat and drink with
tax collectors and sinners?"**—*Luke 5:30*

Jesus did not just speak about the universal reign of God; he lived it
in the most ordinary yet extraordinary way possible: by enjoying
table fellowship with everyone and anyone. All were valued and
welcomed in his presence. He scandalized everyone by refusing to be
scandalized by anyone.

I have vivid memories of one occasion while I was rector of San
Fernando Cathedral in downtown San Antonio. It was the beginning of the spread of AIDS, and I discovered that there was a lot of
prostitution in the downtown area. The people selling their bodies
were part of my flock, and I tried to minister to them as best I could.
The seminary had certainly not prepared me for this, but Jesus' example of sharing his table showed me the way. It was simple and to
the point: befriend them and share table fellowship with them.
Many of the ones I got to know carried deep spiritual wounds of
abuse, abandonment, and betrayal. They were beautiful people who
had suffered unfortunate experiences in life.

As I began to pastor some of these individuals, I discovered why Jesus had such a special place in his heart for such people. Every one of them had incredible stories of pain, rejection, abuse, alienation, abandonment, and suffering. I often befriended them, and they trusted me with their stories. I could not help loving them. It's so easy to condemn when we don't know the facts; it's so easy to moralize when we have not walked the path of another. On a cold winter morning after our 6:00 A.M. Mass, I took a couple of young street persons who had been walking the streets all night exercising their profession to a well-known restaurant for breakfast. Shortly after we sat down at table, the manager called me aside and said, "Father, do you know who those people are?" I was reminded of the criticism made of Jesus: "Why do you eat and drink with tax collectors and sinners?" (Luke 5:30).

Who do you invite to enjoy a meal with you? And whose invitation to dinner are you willing to accept? A delicious meal can become tasteless when you are in the company of boring people and even sickening when in the company of obnoxious ones. Yet even a simple bowl of beans can be the tastiest meal in the world in the company of people you enjoy. Archbishop Patrick Flores has often said that it is not what is on the table that is important, but who is around it! A banquet with the wrong company can seem like an eternity, while a fiesta with fun-loving people passes by as if in an instant.

A festive meal is at one and the same time most beautiful and most revealing of social reality. Who gets invitations, and who is denied entrance? Who sits at table, and who is doing the serving? Who feels welcome, and who feels out of place because of dress, ethnicity, social class, or some other category? I remember some time ago an African American preacher describing heaven as the festive banquet at which everyone is enjoying themselves at table and there are no waiters! A banquet at which there are no distinctions because everyone is equally having a good time! No wonder the joyful table fellowship of Jesus was a foretaste of the fullness of life in heaven.

If Jesus had been around today, enjoying table fellowship with the type of people he enjoyed dining with, I am sure people would have said of him: "*pobre inocente, no sabe con qué tipo de gente se está juntando*" ("poor innocent fool, he doesn't realize what kind of people he is hanging around with"). Yet this type of table companionship was one of the most regular activities of Jesus' early life and one that his followers remembered with such fondness that they continued it as a regular feature of their new existence.

"And people will come . . . and will recline at table in the kingdom of God"—*Luke 13:29*

In the midst of all the wars, ethnic fights, and religious intolerance, wouldn't it be wonderful to create a space where people could be working, living, and celebrating together simply as human beings? The unity of humanity begins not with ideologies but with the experience of togetherness that transcends all the ordinary taboos of segregation. I learned about this at a very early age.

In my father's grocery store in the Mexican neighborhood of San Antonio, Texas, the biggest vegetables, the tastiest fruit, most tender meats, and the best chickens and turkeys were always said to come from my father's ranch and farm, which, because of its many marvels, was known as *La Maravilla*. Even the finest milk, butter, and cheeses were said to come from the wonderful cows and goats of *La Maravilla*. From its reputation, one would certainly get the impression that *La Maravilla* was a huge estate of thousands of acres of the finest grazing lands and the most fertile fields.

Actually, it was only a two-acre piece of land on the outskirts of San Antonio along the banks of the Medina River with nothing more than a few jack rabbits, squirrels, and snakes moving between the cacti, mesquite trees, and other wild shrubs. What gave rise to the very popular myth of the great marvels of *La Maravilla* was not the physical things it produced but the marvelous fellowship that was experienced there.

Every Sunday, *mi Papá* would take a carload of *chorizos*, meats, and chickens to barbecue. There would be plenty of salads, beans, corn on the cob, lemonade, and beer for anyone who wanted to come. My college friends of all ethnic, religious, and social backgrounds would come just as easily as friends from the neighborhood and professional people who were friends of *Papá*. Without any concern for anyone's background or identity, the friendly conversation could easily go from world affairs to neighborhood gossip, to joke telling to anything else. No topic was out of place, and no one ever felt out of place. Whoever came was equally welcomed, and there was always plenty of food and drink for everyone. At *La Maravilla* we were all friends and cared about each other. People came not because they already cared about each other, but in the midst of the fellowship produced by the food and drink they shared in common, they became friends and started to care for one another. This was the community of *La Maravilla*, whose marvels became known as a paradise on earth full of the best things of the earth. In actuality it had only the very best: a community of friends where everyone who came experienced unconditional welcome; a place where strangers became friends, and friends rejoiced in the company of one another.

My dad has been dead for more than thirty years, yet for those who remember, the myth of *La Maravilla* continues to grow and enliven our lives. I suppose that this is where I first experienced the creative force and life-giving joy of table fellowship. The weekly feasts at *La Maravilla* did not seem like anything religious any more than the table parties of Jesus appeared to be a religious celebration. In hindsight I realize, through reflections on the way of Jesus, that I was taking part in the purest of any religious ritual: the joy of inclusive table fellowship and a foretaste of the eternal banquet in heaven at the end of time.

As I reflect on the way of Jesus, I realize more and more that what made *La Maravilla* so special was that it was indeed sacred space: a space where everyone was welcomed and radically accepted not for their titles, ethnicity, or social class but simply because they were human beings! This is the great marvel of the irruption of the reign of God and a foretaste of the heavenly fiesta in the fullness of time.

"Jesus did this [changed water into wine] as the beginning of his signs"—*John 2:11*

The first of the many miracles Jesus performed was at Cana of Galilee during a wedding feast. Jesus performed many other miracles, but I think that the most significant of the new life he was living and offering to everyone was turning water into wine at the wedding feast in Cana.

Wedding feasts in those days were very much like our small-town family wedding fiestas, where there is plenty of food, drink, conversation, music, and dancing and everyone, young and old, rich and poor, has a great time together. Jesus wanted the good time to continue. He had come to proclaim the good news of the reign of God, and what a great way to begin! He had come to bring people together so that they might experience the joy of being together—indeed a great marvel in our segregated and divided world.

He could easily have said, "I have more important things to do. . . . I have much more urgent things to worry about. There are lots of poor among the people; let's get on to feeding them. There are lots of sick people around; let's get on to curing them." But no, he was enjoying himself, saw how everyone else was having a great time, and wanted the feast to continue. Indeed, healings would take place, the poor would receive plenty, and the downtrodden would be uplifted; Mary had already predicted this (Luke 1:51–53). But the greatest healing of all would be the reunification of humanity into one loving human family. The good news of Jesus was not an apocalyptic end but a joyful beginning. The marvelous miracle was not only the first sign that Jesus performed but also the most significant, for it marked the beginning and set the tone for the new alternative humanity that Jesus was now inaugurating: the festive joy of a new togetherness. This was a great way to inaugurate the new Messianic times.

Jesus not only proclaimed the new alternative of the reign of God; he lived it in the most ordinary yet shocking way. Throughout the rest of his public ministry, Jesus would scandalize the righteous and saintly while inspiring the poor and the lowly by his joyful table fellowship with the so-called public sinners of his time. "While he was at table in his house, many tax collectors and sinners came and sat with Jesus and his disciples" (Matthew 9:10).

Joyful table fellowship with anyone and everyone was one of the most regular aspects of the life and ministry of Jesus, and it was without doubt what caused the greatest furor. John the Baptist and his disciples, like the Pharisees and other holiness groups, fasted while Jesus and his followers feasted! One was the way of penance; the other was the way of fiesta. "And they said to him, 'The disciples of John fast often and offer prayers, and the disciples of the Pharisees do the same; but yours eat and drink'" (Luke 5:33). I often wonder how many of our Christian church services today truly resemble this joyful table fellowship of Jesus.

There is an irony in this all-inclusive community that Jesus is initiating. It is scandalous and dangerous to those who have held the monopoly on status and belonging, to the custodians of the status quo. Their rules and customs are de-authorized and rendered ineffective. Everyone is now invited, but not everyone will come. Many will stay away not because they are not invited but precisely because now everyone is invited. Those who have had the privileged invitations to the places of worldly prestige and honor will not want to mix and rub shoulders with the insignificant and "worthless" people of society. They will indeed be invited, as in the parable of the great wedding feast of Luke 14:15–24, but they will offer silly excuses why they cannot come. Thus, because Jesus rejects exclusion, some will choose to exclude themselves!

Why was this seemingly superficial activity of Jesus so meaningful to his followers that they would continue to practice it long before there was any theology of Eucharist and so offensive to his critics that they would drive him to the cross? Why was it so fundamental for the new creation which Jesus was inaugurating?

Up until now, humanity had developed through "divide and conquer," and division was in the air everywhere. Societies had all kinds of categories by which to exclude those who were unwanted, just as societies today have all kinds of ways of marking people as untouchables and unwanted. The unwanted are kept out in many diverse ways. Just witness how we in the United States keep out the immigrant poor we don't want around, or we allow them in to do the work nobody else wants to do and then chase them out. We still live in a world of exclusion, which denies the basic dignity and infinite worth of millions of fellow human beings. Because those in power categorize the defenseless, the poor, and the weak as unwanted, we deny them the basic right of belonging. Even when they make their way in, they are still excluded from many of the activities of the dominant group, most especially their social gatherings and wedding feasts. Segregation and exclusion are all the worse when they are done in the name of divine righteousness, in the name of God!

As if it was not enough that in Jesus of Nazareth God became the outcast of a sinful world, this outcast would now shock and scandalize many of the respectable people of his time because he would eat and drink with everyone without exception, especially the excluded persons of his time. But it was much more than that. The people of his time were convinced that the expected and anticipated reign of God could not be born as long as there were "public sinners" among them. It was precisely because of the impure outcasts and public sinners that the reign of God was prevented from arriving. Now, in the very name of God, who is father of all, the outcasts and excluded were not only invited into the banquet but their inclusion was said to be a sign of the actual arrival of God's reign: "I say to you, many will come from the east and the west and will recline at table with Abraham, Isaac and Jacob at the banquet in the kingdom of heaven" (Matthew 8:11). The joyful table fellowship of Jesus that so angered his own people was in fact a foretaste and anticipation of the new universalism that Jesus came to inaugurate.

The opening of the public ministry of Jesus with the wedding feast at Cana is the inauguration of the new space of universal belonging, and it points to that activity which will be most characteristic of the earthly Jesus and of the early Christian movement: the joy of table fellowship, the joy that burns in the heart of everyone being welcomed! The miracle turns the continuation of the feast itself—with the water converted into delicious wine—into a powerful parable about the nature of the Kingdom of God which Jesus came to inaugurate. It draws attention to all the activity of Jesus culminating in the Last Supper, where the wine will now be converted into the drink of the everlasting life. It was a great way to begin and an exciting sign of things to come.

For many of us today, the conversion of the bitter water into the best of wine was not only the first of the many miracles, but a symbol of the conversion of the bitterness of segregation and exclusion into the sweetness of unity and inclusion. This is the beginning of a new alternative world to the empires the world had built and continues to build, empires of exclusion, segregation, and exploitation of the weak and defenseless, where artificial pleasures, far from producing real inner and lasting joy, result in an ever-deepening emptiness, loneliness, and alienation. No wonder people in the empires of the world have such a great need for psychoanalysis, tranquilizers, sleeping pills, and the like. The empires of the world, with all of their wealth and technology, cannot give what God alone can give: the fullness of life, but only if we listen to Mary's words: "do whatever he tells you" (John 2:5).

No wonder the miracle in favor of the continuation of the feast is the first of the many signs Jesus was to perform. And he did indeed perform many wondrous deeds. But the one that I find most fascinating and that probably led him to the cross the fastest was his willingness and ability to have a good time with anyone and everyone. This was most meaningful to his followers and most infuriating to his critics. In this he scandalized many, because he refused to be scandalized by anyone. "The Pharisees and their scribes complained to his disciples, saying, 'Why do you eat and drink with tax collectors?'" (Luke 5:30).

"This is my body, which will be given for you"—*Luke 22:19*

The Christian tradition has always celebrated the intimate connection between the last table fellowship of Jesus and his sacrifice on the cross. As powerful as the sacrifice on the cross is, it cannot be isolated from his lifetime practice of sacrificing himself, especially his reputation, for the sake of others. In his ordinary practice of all-inclusive table fellowship, he gave himself to us in the most intimate way possible. In the proximity of eating together at the common table, his body came into contact with the bodies of others. Barriers of contamination and separation were ignored as the new family of the spirit was gestating. Neither blood nor social status would matter, for a new blood would now run through the veins of the new community of brothers and sisters. But Jesus would have to pay a very high price to bring this about.

The preparation for his ultimate sacrifice was his willingness to sacrifice his social status, reputation, and even his credibility by becoming friends with the social outcasts and public sinners of his world. We say in Spanish, "Dime con quién andas, y te diré quién eres" ("Tell me who you hang around with, and I will tell you who you are"). He was not only friends with them, he even enjoyed eating and drinking with them. He was not ashamed to be seen fraternizing with anyone, regardless of their reputation or social status. Jesus was the totally free person who would not hold back from doing God's will because of public opinion or the immoral customs that had become socially accepted to the degree that they were enforced in the name of God.

Table fellowship was indeed the festive beginning, the body and soul experience of the reign of God, a festive space in which everyone will be welcomed and treated alike without regard to what others (society or religion) say that you are. The joy of being welcomed and appreciated unconditionally is experienced by those who wine and dine with Jesus, and this was already, even before the cross and resurrection, the first buds of the springtime of a new humanity, a humanity like the world had never known. As biblical scholar Norman Perrin has noted, "The 'table fellowship of the kingdom,' as we have called it, was a feature of the common life of Jesus and his followers altogether, and a symbol of the new kind of relationships made possible by the common acceptance of the challenge. Scribe, tax-collector, fisherman and Zealot came together around the table at which they celebrated the joy of the present experience and anticipated its consummation in the future" (Perrin 1976, p. 107).

The greatest miracle of Jesus—one that has not been looked upon as a miracle and yet it is the one that the very first Christians remembered with such fondness that they continued practicing it daily—was his joy of radically inclusive table fellowship. In his company, strangers became friends and foreigners became blood family. Jesus loved to have a good time with close friends and with anyone and everyone. This was not a one-time affair. In fact, it was so regular and ordinary during the earthly life of Jesus that the early Christians who wanted to follow his way made it the greatest characteristic of their own new life. This is what attracted so many to join the new group. It was not just new teachings about God, but the new experience of a unifying God who could bring all people together in a festive and loving way.

Jesus brings his earthly ministry to completion in a very similar way in which he started: a festive meal with his friends. What has come to be known as the last supper was precisely that, the last of what had been most regular in the life of Jesus. In this final festive meal, Jesus gives us the connection between the ongoing sacrifice of his life for the sake of the inclusion of others to the final sacrifice which will be demanded of him by those who opposed this radical desegregation of humanity in the name of the God who is Father of all. Yet even when they got rid of him on the cross, they could not put a stop to the new practice of festive-inclusive meals that in turn gave rise to new social relations and concerns for the welfare of one another.

After the resurrection, Jesus gives instructions to his disciples that they are to go to Galilee, and there they will see him. They did so, and one early morning after they had been fishing all night and catching nothing, Jesus appeared and told them to cast the net on the other side, very much like at Cana, telling them to do something that humanly speaking did not make sense. But they did it and caught a huge amount; so huge that their nets were on the point of breaking. While they were doing this, Jesus was on the shore nearby preparing breakfast for them, an early-morning barbecue for his friends. In the context of this simple yet festive meal with his followers, Jesus asks Peter: "Do you love me?" (John 21:15). He did not ask Peter: "Do you now understand everything I have taught you?" or "Will you now be strong enough not to deny me again?" or "Do you think you have the proper qualities to lead my followers?" He simply asks him in the very context of table fellowship, "Do you love me?" Peter answers in the affirmative and is thus commissioned to lead the flock. Yes, it is not through authoritarian power that we are to lead but through loving service, creating spaces in the midst of empires wherein everyone will be welcomed, recognized, accepted, and valued. Like Jesus, we will scandalize those who defend exclusive domains that exclude others under various excuses and practical reasons. But we, following in the steps of our Master, will continue to find new ways of building an alternative world wherein nobody will be excluded and we will continue beginning where Jesus began: in the festive meals to which all are invited.

Jesus performed many miraculous deeds and spoke many fascinating words during his lifetime. But none was more marvelous than his ordinary practice of having a good time with anyone and everyone especially around one of the most intimate moments of life: table fellowship.

"Come to me, all you who labor and are burdened, and I will give you rest"—*Matthew 11:28*

I have learned a lot from my Latino university students. One of the fascinating things that they have taught me is that the main reason they like to go to church is because it is a place to "hang around" and meet new friends. Many of these students come from poverty-ridden areas and would not feel at home anywhere else; but on the church grounds, they feel accepted and welcomed. Here their dignity is recognized and affirmed. They do not have to explain to anyone why they are who they are, but can simply be and know they are welcomed. They do not like to just "go to church" (that is, go to Mass); they like to come and hang around.

To me this is very reflective of how the crowds loved to hang around Jesus, even forgetting where they were to eat. The sacred space created by Jesus is not an other-worldly experience but definitely a transworldly one. The ordinary phenomena of exclusion and put-down are (or should be) nonexistent within the church grounds. Here there are no "illegals," marginals, or untouchables, for everyone is welcomed in the household of the Lord.

Church is important not just for its liturgies but because it is a "sacred space" where all kinds of people can come together, become friends, and discover a new life. There is no fear of rejection in the spaces created by Jesus. It is a place where people can socialize equally whether they are bankers, janitors, homeless, mansion dwellers, doctors, or unemployed. You never know who you will meet in church and start a friendship with that can easily change your life. It is this space of conviviality that makes our churches an experience of the kingdom of God, a foretaste of the great fiesta that will come at the end of time. We tried to create such a sacred space at San Fernando Cathedral by ensuring that everyone without exception would feel equally welcomed: millionaire or street person, citizen or undocumented, Catholic or anything else. Dan Groody did just this at Grand Central Station when in a small but most significant way he created a sacred space by recognizing, valuing, and in a way feasting with a simple cup of coffee a woman who had been ignored by the thousands who passed by.

Today this invitation of Jesus to all who are tired and burdened becomes all the more important to Christians in the United States as we are called upon to welcome the poor of the world who are tired of their misery and burdened with the harsh conditions of life in their countries. We find it exciting and romantic to send missioners into foreign countries, but often find it very difficult to accept and welcome incoming immigrants, especially if they are poor, into our communities. Yet this is precisely what Christianity is about: welcoming the poor, the unwanted, and the rejected into the fellowship of God's love. The first missionary command of Jesus is "Come to me" (Matthew 11:28). Only then, when we have become a welcoming community, are we ready for the second missionary command: "Go to all nations" (Matthew 28:19).

The festive fellowship of Jesus, continued in the Christian community, is the beginning, the foretaste, and the sign of the kingdom of God in its fullness. As beautiful as it is, because of the diabolic powers still active and operative both around us and within us, it will continue to emerge only at the cost of great sacrifice. It will not come about through the offering of external sacrifices, but through the voluntary self-sacrifice of those who have experienced the love of God in Christ and are willing, like Jesus, to sacrifice their social status, reputation, security, and even their lives for the sake of others.

¡VIVA LA FIESTA!

~

CHAPTER NINE

The Beauty of Sacrifice

**"If you believe, you will see
the glory of God"**—*John 11:40*

The witness of artists, poets, musicians, and most of all our ancestors is dramatic in how it is able to see and portray the glory of God in spite of gruesome, cruel, and bloody events.

One of the very obvious and pervasive expressions of mestizo Christianity in Latin America is the presence of *Nazarenos* in the churches, public shrines, and homes. Very realistic images of the scourged and bleeding Jesus crowned with thorns are found everywhere and continue to be reproduced by artists and proclaimed by singers. It is a favorite image of prisoners, as if it says "he is with us in our incarceration." It is a favorite image of the masses of the poor who see in the suffering and bleeding God a God who has not abandoned them in their suffering. It is not a glorification of suffering but a recognition that even in the worst of suffering, God is with us. Even when we are a scandal to others, God becomes a scandal with us so that we are never alone.

The crucifixes that hang in homes and shrines are also realistic, so realistic that they are often shocking to many. Many, especially in societies of wealth and power, would rather see the beautiful body of a perfect model on the cross rather than that of a human being disfigured by the cruelty of others. How could such a one be a savior of humanity?

Nowhere else has the Christian tradition of the suffering and self-sacrifice of Jesus blended more beautifully with the ancient Mexican tradition of the suffering and self-sacrifice of Quetzalcoatl than in the popular wisdom of the common people expressed through their popular art, songs, devotions, *dichos*, and rituals. Through Jesus, the best and purest of ancient Mexican wisdom emerged gloriously from the past, but equally through the ancient wisdom of our ancestors, the people were able to grasp the deepest and most beautiful meaning of the redemptive suffering and sacrifice of Jesus—a life lived entirely for the sake of others, even to the point of giving one's life so that others might live.

Yet this beautiful wisdom of our native Mexican ancestors was coupled with the cosmic worldview of succeeding generations that believed in an obligation to nourish the sun with the most precious liquid of all, human blood, so that the sun would not be extinguished and humanity would survive. Jesus redeemed the native Mexican religions from their need to practice human sacrifice for the sake of cosmic survival while at the same time illuminating and deepening their own sense of the value of self-sacrifice for the sake of others. The people's ancient sense of the salvific value and beauty of sacrifice, of the value of the body and blood given for the sake of the world, continues to offer universal Christianity a realistic remembrance and presence of the full reality of the crucifixion of Jesus for our salvation.

The reasons for ancient Mexican sacrifice and Jesus' sacrifice were similar in that they were both offered for the salvation of humanity. But otherwise they were totally different. For the ancient Mexicans, the sun, the source of all nature, needed to be nourished with the mystical source of life within human beings: the pulsating heart and blood. They sacrificed human beings for the survival of earth and humanity.

For Jesus, it was humanity's sin that was destroying earth and humanity. Through humanity's sinful actions, all of nature had been contaminated and needed redemption. Nature did not need to be nourished by the physical sacrifice of human hearts, but all of creation needed to be re-created by loving hearts. It would not be through human sacrifice of others but through a new force: loving others unconditionally, even at the cost of death. It wasn't nature that needed to be nourished by human hearts, but human hearts that needed to be nourished by love—loving hearts that would rehabilitate all of creation.

I suspect this is the deepest root of the originality of the Latin American mestizo Christian tradition. The figure of Quetzalcoatl did not believe in the sacrifice of others. He practiced self-discipline for the sake of harmony with his own self, with others, and with the cosmic order. For him, harmony, what we Christians would call "community," was the essence of life. The mythical Quetzalcoatl sacrificed himself so that, by throwing himself into the fire, human beings might be born. Through his self-sacrifice, the new creation of the *Quinto Sol* ("Fifth Sun") was begun. The ongoing voluntary sacrifice of self was not only the very essence of life but generative of life itself. It was only later civilizations that developed the notion of the need of human sacrifice to assure the survival of the cosmos.

The mutuality of interpretation between this ancient image wisdom of the Mexicans and message of the crucifixion-sacrifice of Jesus is the ongoing life source of Mexican spirituality. It is expressed in many ways, transmitted through many forms, and celebrated in passionate rituals. In this very radical acceptance of life as it is, even in its most painful moments, there is already the beginning of an experience of resurrection.

Theologians insist on the importance of the resurrection of Jesus as the ultimate and greatest manifestation of his Lordship, and they are right. As St. Paul states, if Christ had not risen, our faith is in vain (1 Corinthians 15:17). Easter Sunday without Good Friday is empty, but Good Friday without Easter Sunday is senseless. Yet it is the crucifixion and the events around it that have inspired the greatest works of art and continues to do so today. They see beyond the surface and bring out the unsuspected beauty of what is hidden by the externals. Our *Nahua* ancestors used to think that the artists were persons with God-possessed hearts who could intuit divine truth and express it through beauty. This certainly seems to be the case when interpreting the sacrifice of Jesus. It is as if the artists intuit the innermost beauty of sacrifice for the sake of others even unto death, even a cruel and shameful death.

In religious goods stores the crucifix outnumbers images of the resurrection (which are usually not very good) by a hundred to one. People seek the crucifix, for it reveals the ultimate beauty of our God who loved us so much, even in our sinfulness, that he not only became one of us, but entered into solidarity with the victims of unjust structures and even went to the extreme of giving his life for us so that a new way of life might be introduced into humanity.

The execution of a person condemned for a crime is never a beautiful or inspiring event, although in our sinful perversity people seem to be excited and even entertained by public executions. Lynchings in the United States were popular gatherings with a festive spirit. It was not uncommon for schools to let out and even church services to be interrupted so that the people could join in the carnival spirit of the lynching. Such executions might be entertaining in a perverse sort of way, but they are never inspiring. Yet the execution of Jesus on the cross in the most cruel way possible has not only inspired artists but moved people even to martyrdom. From the very beginning it inspired the Roman centurion, who was accustomed to seeing divinity only in Caesar, to exclaim, "truly this was the son of God" (Matthew 27:54). Another version of the event renders it this way: "This man was innocent beyond doubt" (Luke 23:47). In the very way he died, not only was his complete innocence revealed but even more so his divinity apparent. Today, it continues to inspire not only fine art and classical music but barrio art, Third World art, and prison art. It is amazing how the image of something so cruel, especially when seen in the context of the entire life of Jesus, can continue to inspire not only beautiful art but beautiful behavior of heroic dimensions.

"My kingdom does not belong to this world"—*John 18:36*

Around San Fernando Cathedral in San Antonio and in many of the towns throughout Latin America, there is no greater and more beautiful day than Good Friday. This is the day when we proclaim Jesus as *El Señor del Poder* ("The God of Power). No day of the year brings more people together at one time than the reenactment of the trial, crucifixion, and burial of Jesus. In a way, the vale of time and space is removed and the events of the first Good Friday take place in the here and now today—and we are present at this great moment of history. I have experienced this many times, and it never fails to move me deeply and to inspire me to recommit myself to the following of Jesus, no matter the cost. As a human being and as a pastor, this is truly the most beautiful, most moving, and most inspiring day of the year.

All the celebrations of Easter pale in comparison to the celebration of *Viernes Santo* (Good Friday). No Easter Vigil liturgy, no matter how beautifully planned and executed, can compare to the divine beauty that shines forth throughout the day on Viernes Santo. Many tend to see our Mexican celebrations as gruesome. Some see them as a sick spirit that enshrines cruelty and bloodshed. But for the poor and suffering of the world, the silent victims of the world's systemic cruelty, the crucified peoples of today's world, it is the beautiful day of the ultimate triumph of God's love over the evil forces of this world. It is the day when we see and experience the true face and heart of God, who is not ashamed of being with us in our multiple humiliations and suffering and who even becomes himself the suffering victim of the world's cruelty. In his triumph over evil in all its cultural and religious expressions, our own triumph is guaranteed. It is truly the glorification of divine love made visible through the unlimited love of Jesus, even unto the sacrifice of the cross.

The people come to the Viernes Santo reenactment on crutches, in wheelchairs, babies in arms, children in hand. It is the most important religious event for the poor. During Viernes Santo, it is as if we are all together taking part in the original events in Jerusalem. The ultimate religious symbol of Christianity is intermingled with the living reality of the peoples for an astounding mutuality of interpretation and enrichment. In this very living-out of Christian imagery through human reality, new life irrupts both collectively and in each one of the participants.

"Jesus said to Peter, 'Put your sword into its scabbard. Shall I not drink the cup that the Father gave me?'"—*John 18:11*

On this day, the people spontaneously proclaim the powerless, scourged man carrying the cross as "The Lord of Power," for it is precisely in his power to endure the insults and physical torments without losing his dignity, self-composure, or inner strength that he reveals the power of God to overcome violence without giving into violence. Violence will never eradicate violence. It is in his apparent powerlessness that the ultimate power of love is revealed. It is this power of endurance for the sake of life that characterizes the life and struggles of the Latin American poor. Without this power, we would no longer be in existence today. Outsiders see this as fatalism; we see it as the power of love to triumph over the diabolical powers of injustice of this world. Because of sin, this world belongs to Satan; but through love, Jesus will win it for God: "Jesus answered, 'My kingdom does not belong to this world. If my kingdom did belong to this world, my attendants [would] be fighting to keep me from being handed over to the Jews. But as it is, my kingdom is not here'" (John 18:36).

Christ will reign over the world, but it will not be a reign of power, domination, and control. The reign of Christ will be of an entirely different nature. It is the reign where "He has shown might with his arm, dispersed the arrogant of mind and heart. He has thrown down the rulers from their thrones but lifted up the lowly. The hungry he has filled with good things; the rich he has sent away empty" (Luke 1:51–53).

Good Friday is the day of the poor, the lowly, and the insignificant of this world. It is the day of the rejected and of those falsely accused; it is the day of the unwanted and tormented of this world. This is the day in which we proclaim what is ultimately sacred to us in the way that is truly meaningful to us. At no time is the sacredness of our struggles and of our ability to endure no matter what for the sake of the new life more forceful and inspiring than during the living events of Good Friday. Like Jesus, we defy public opinion and liturgical rituals as we proudly walk with him carrying his cross down our *Via Dolorosa*. In the passion and death of Jesus, God enters fully into our own way of the cross, into our own struggles for life, dignity, and freedom. We are not ashamed to be with our God no matter how disgraced, disfigured, and rejected he is by human society. In the way of the cross, God accompanies us and even takes our place in our most excruciating situations of life. In the crucified word made flesh, our own tragedies take on a new life and signification: "Then they crucified him and divided his garments by casting lots for them to see what each should take" (Mark 15:24).

Everything was taken away from Jesus as he was left naked on the cross. He was truly stripped of all dignity and presented in a humiliating way to the world. We have to remember that everything—everything!—is taken away from the victims, as was the case with the Africans who were forced to come to the Americas to serve as slaves; the natives of this land who lost their properties, their families, their honor, and their dignity; the victims of the Holocaust, who were stripped of everything before being taken to their execution; and today's victims of individual or social injustices. They are falsely judged and condemned, scourged, crowned with thorns, nailed to the crosses of harsh work, and crucified naked, deprived of even the most minimum of human dignity. This is the everyday lot of the victims of injustice then and today: the undocumented worker, the campesinos, the farmworkers, the ex-prisoners, the domestic workers, the *maquiladora* workers, the prostitutes, the day laborers. They are deprived of dignity, credibility, or human worth of any kind.

The public agony of Jesus is merely the bringing out into the public of the hidden suffering and misery of the victims of society. His cries for life from the cross are the cries for life of those whom society has silenced, now being heard by everyone. Through Jesus, the poor, the silenced, and the suffering of the world dare to proclaim to all that we are human beings, that we are here, that we are someone (not just statistics), that we are alive. It is a call to everyone to hear the cries of the innocent victims of our selfish and individualistic society who are eager to bring to an end any and every type of victimization.

"The hour has come for the Son of Man to be glorified"—*John 12:23*

Throughout his life, Jesus took many risks in confronting the many traditions, customs, and regulations that kept people from appreciating their full dignity as children of God. He was often questioned, insulted, and threatened. But now, it would appear that he had been defeated and his life would come to a horrible end. Or would it? "When Jesus had said this, he raised his eyes to heaven and said, 'Father, the hour has come. Give glory to your son, so that your son may glorify you'" (John 17:1).

Many have wondered why this cruel and bloody execution has become a religious symbol of such magnitude. Why is something so horrible the most beautiful symbol of Christianity? Why would good and religious people do such a thing? Why would such ugliness become such beauty?

It is in flesh and blood solidarity with the crucified of today's world that we can see and begin to understand what the crucifixion of Jesus continues to reveal about God, humanity, and each one of us. Today's crucified peoples are the contemporary interpreters of the original event. Far from being the tragic end of a good man's life, the crucifixion generated one of the most incredible paradoxes of history: the execution of a condemned criminal by the justice of sinful society became a life-giving force for millions of persons of all ages, races, and regions of the world; one of the ugliest spectacles would become one of the most beautiful and life-giving sights.

The actual passion and crucifixion of Jesus, the ultimate revelation of the beauty of God's love, may appear as something completely profane and completely distant from any of our notions of the sacred. In the crucifixion we do not see the omnipotent God who frees his people from the powerful Pharaoh or the all-powerful armies of any nation vanquishing the enemy by a greater force. Instead it is the apparently powerless God who is impotent in relation to the powers of the world. In the crucified Jesus we do not see the towering figure of Moses leading the people out of the enslavement of Egypt, or Joshua capturing the promised land, or Solomon reigning over the majestic city of Jerusalem but an apparently defeated man stripped even of his most basic dignity.

I will never forget the question of a third-grade student who asked me, "Father, why did God allow those evil men to kill his son? Couldn't he stop them?" From the mouths of infants flow the most challenging questions. My theology of humanity's sin demanding the sacrifice of the divine-human son to appease the anger of the Father just didn't make sense. I knew then that we had to probe deeper into the reason for the crucifixion. A loving God just could not be that vengeful. I certainly could not believe in such a God.

At first sight, in the crucifixion we see a Father who was not able to protect his only son from the powerful mechanisms of the evil of this world. But behind what we see is a much deeper reality—a God parent who is so disgusted with the ways of violence of his very own creation that he empowered the Son to resist and destroy violence without using violence of any kind. This indeed is something totally new: the idea that someone would love so much that he would give his life rather than take someone else's. Jesus triumphed not by taking anyone's life, but by offering his own for the sake of others. He triumphed not by defeating violence with a greater violence, which our modern media glorifies, but by continuing to love regardless of the violence inflicted upon him. This was a new and unsuspected force. This is the ultimate beauty and power of the sacrifice of the cross. Truly, this was the hour of his glorification!

"You have the words of eternal life"—*John 6:68*

At the worst moment in the life of Jesus, he speaks the most beautiful words. At the moment when an earthquake was taking place (Matthew 27:51), Jesus speaks the words that continue to produce earthquakes in the very ground of our personal being to allow new life to burst forth from the tombs of social death.

"Father, forgive them, they know not what they do"—*Luke 23:33–34*

From the throne of his cathedral, Jesus proclaimed the most beautiful and powerful word of life. In a world poisoned and torn apart by violence, vengeance, betrayals, abandonments, insults, and indifference, forgiveness is the only way to inner freedom, peace, and tranquillity. Holding grudges enslaves and embitters; forgiveness liberates and restores life. Without forgiveness, life is worse than death, and death is eternal torment. Jesus lived in such a world. He was betrayed, abused, and abandoned. Yet he lived to forgive. For only in forgiveness is even death dissolved into life everlasting, and previous pains transformed unto unending joy. To forgive is to live.

"Today you shall be with me in Paradise"—*Luke 23:43*

Is there one of us who has not failed in some way or another? Is there one of us that at sometime has not been a criminal deserving of punishment? "I've done nothing wrong!" Denial is as great a curse as unending self-flagellation, "I deserve it!" Acting as if no wrong had been committed is as great a sickness as the constant torments of guilt. But unquestioned trust in the one who dies for us rehabilitates anyone. As always, Jesus has the way to inner healing: simply admit your guilt, trust in him, and God will do the rest! "Today, you will be with me in paradise."

"Woman, behold, your son . . . Behold, your mother"—*John 19:26–27*

No one should ever be left alone or unattended. The best insurance policy, the best orphanage, the best nursing home will not suffice without personal care and tenderness. To be humanly alive, we need to be concerned for others and know that others are concerned about us, to love and be loved. Not even death should separate us from those we love, from those who in life have given us life. Jesus' physical agony on the cross is overcome and transcended by his compassion, by his tender care for those around him. Others can nail his body to the cross, but they cannot hold him back from loving others on earth and beyond. Only in caring for others does our own suffering become submerged in the peacefulness of eternal life—not the life of the hereafter, but the beginning of eternal life that is found in today's bonds of loving concern and care.

"My God, my God, why have you foresaken me?"—*Matthew 27:46*

What an incredible love Jesus showed for all of us! For there is no greater love than to share in the deepest agony of the beloved. Jesus, in his own body and spirit, shared our excruciating pains of embarrassment, shame, failure, alienation, loneliness, and distress. Because of this unlimited love for us, God has raised him to eternal life. When I feel totally down in the affairs of life, I need not fear and I need not despair. For I know that the son of God is with me to give me that hope beyond all human hope, that God—no mere human—will triumph in me. In the abandonment of Jesus, I am rescued from my own abandonment. For God is with me no matter what.

"I Thirst"—*John 19:28*

Jesus was condemned by his people and abandoned by his friends. The thousands who had wanted to make him king had now demanded his death. When all goes well, we have plenty of friends and followers; when we fail, we are quickly maligned and abandoned. Those that were proud of us quickly become ashamed of having known us. Those who had received favors quickly throw mud. The loneliness of condemnation, shame, and abandonment is a worse torment than death. The deepest thirst of the human spirit is not for drink but for understanding, acceptance, and accompaniment. Only we can offer this drink of life that will quench the deepest thirst of the human heart parched by rejection and abandonment.

"It Is Finished!"—*John 19:30*

"I have conquered the world" (John 16:33). This statement is not a recognition of defeat, but an affirmation of triumph. The beautiful satisfaction of the artist, the scientist, the architect, the cook, the janitor, the parent, the teacher—those who have worked hard, struggled through the many unsuspected difficulties, suffered the misunderstanding and maybe even ridicule of others and apparent failure but have remained faithful in bringing the project to completion. Jesus remained absolutely faithful to God's project for humanity: to love others no matter the cost, no matter the response, "so that they may all be one." Throughout his entire life and most of all in these final moments, he had made visible the very structure and essence of true love. Truly, a loving heart has reasons that reason alone will never understand! Our task is not to win approval, but to love no matter what. All our power and might could not destroy the force of his love. In spite of the most scandalous denunciations and gruesome attacks, he remained steadfast. Others thought he had failed in disgrace, but he shouted a spontaneous cry of gratitude, triumph, and victory at his death: "It's finished . . . it is finally complete!" Death is not the end of life, but merely the completion of life's project, which, like every great piece of art, continues to live forever.

"Father, into Your Hands I Commend My Spirit"—*Luke 23:46*

What a beautiful way to depart from this world, with complete confidence in the God of life. Even in dying, Jesus is introducing us to the tenderness and unending care of the God of life. No matter what life has in store for me, I need never despair, for no matter what, God is with me and into God's hands I entrust my life and my destiny. What is there left for me to do? Like Jesus, I can enter into the profound satisfaction and blissful peacefulness of knowing that I have done my best in living God's will, and God asks nothing more. God wills that I might live life to the fullest and, in seeking to do God's will, I come to the fullness of life both here and in eternity. For those who are faithful to God's way of love, even if we should die, we need not fear, for we shall live forever.

Having said his final words, having completed his mission faithfully till the bitter end, he gave forth the Spirit. It is most interesting that the gospel stories never say that Jesus died; they say he expired (Mark 15:37 and Luke 23:46), he let go the spirit (Matthew 27:50), bowing his head, and he gave over the spirit (John 19:30). Raymond Brown, in his classic work *The Death of the Messiah* (vol. 2) presented a beautiful intuition regarding bowing the head and giving the spirit. It could well have been that Jesus, bowing his head to look at the faithful who had remained with him, who had not abandoned him, and who were standing at the foot of the cross, gives *them* the spirit. They who followed him unto the cross are the first ones to receive the promised spirit. This is the incredible beauty of this moment, what John calls the hour of the glorification. Just when the world thought they had killed him, he passed to a greater life that no one can destroy or bring to an end while giving his own life source to those standing at the foot of the cross. Humanity had killed him, thought him dead, but he was more alive than ever. His earthly life had come to an end, but his life had not come to an end! This is the glorious beauty that comes through the artistic representations of the crucified—crucified but still giving life and hope to humanity.

"Truly this man was the Son of God . . . an innocent man"—Mark 15:39, Luke 23:47

Paradoxical as it is, the ugliness of the cross reveals the beauty of Jesus, its cruelty reveals the power of his endurance, and its scandal reveals his glory. No wonder that the very moment of his death, his real and ultimate identity was immediately recognized by a centurion calloused by wars and killings: "Truly this was the Son of God" (Matthew 27:54). In the very way Jesus endured the insults of society and even his execution, Jesus arose over the destructive and dehumanizing powers of evil. This was not a fatalistic acceptance of the status quo, but rather the triumph over the ordinary dynamics of violence, which so dominate both the world and the personal behavior of individuals, for the sake of peace, order, and well-being. In his very death, Jesus appears as the innocent victim of the world's injustice, the Son of God on the cross, and the author of the new life of the Spirit.

CHAPTER TEN

~

A Dying Gift

"Behold, your son"—*John 19:26*

In reflecting on the gospel according to John, one could easily say that it is the gospel of the mother. In the gospel according to Luke, the first and last words of Jesus are about the Father: "Why were you looking for me? Did you not know that I must be in my Father's house?" (Luke 2:49). "Father, into your hands I commend my spirit" (Luke 23:46). However, in John's gospel account, it is his mother who gets him started at the wedding feast at Cana, and at the end of his life on earth, when he had done everything he had to do, Jesus gives us his final and most tender gift. From the cross he gives us his own mother to be our mother. If in life he had given us the Our Father, now as his last gift, he gives us the Our Mother. "Then he said to the disciple, 'Behold, your mother.' And from that hour the disciple took her into his home" (John 19:27). The meaning is clear and has been intuited by Christians from the very beginning. There is no Christian family without Mary, the Mother of Jesus and now our own mother, as the unifying and compassionate center of the new family of God.

Jesus knew human nature better than anyone else, and he knew that nothing unites a family more than a loving mother. We need the providential and loving care of a father, but the love and accompaniment of the very one that brought us to life from within her womb provide a bond of unity that is beyond human words to explain. It is not irrational, but it is certainly beyond reason to fully comprehend.

There is no doubt that the bond between mother and children is very strong in Latino cultures. It is so strong that even the toughest guys are like putty in the presence of their mothers. Hence it should not be surprising that Latino Catholicism is very Mary centered. Some have even stated that it is more Marian than Christian. I do not believe this to be the case. In fact, I think our Latino religion, which is based on the two key icons of Mary and Jesus, is much closer to the Christianity of the Gospels than other expressions of Christianity that do not appreciate the incredible and fascinating bond between the mother and her son. This is a bond that becomes all the more powerful in their suffering together for our salvation. Actually this devotion has been present since the earliest days of Christianity. This bond is so close that I would dare to call them a redeeming team.

When people think of Mexican Catholicism, they immediately think of Our Lady of Guadalupe, and they are not wrong. However there are other expressions of Mary that might be less evident but probably are even more powerful. Especially preeminent among them is the devotion to the sorrowful mother.

Unfortunately the great masses of Latinos are among the poor and marginal of society. As *indios*, mestizos, mulattoes and Afro-Latinos they are constantly abused and insulted in many ways. They suffer the prejudices of the dominant society, the misery of economic poverty, and the incarceration and quick death penalties of the defenseless. One of the great sources of strength has been the unconditional love and support of our mothers. We easily see in the suffering mother of Jesus the suffering of our own mothers, who have struggled with us and for us and have never abandoned us. Only a suffering mother can comprehend and appreciate our pains and our sufferings. In the sorrowful mother we see the apparently frail women who in actuality are towers of strength. They are the most incredible life givers and life sustainers anyone could ever imagine.

Mary did not justify, approve, or condone the ugly injustices hurdled against her son, but even if nothing else was possible, she did not abandon him in his moments of greatest need. She stayed with him and stood by him even when others had abandoned him. These are our mothers who stay with their children even when they are unjustly condemned to death. These are our mothers who stay behind in impoverished villages while their children migrate to seek jobs, knowing well that some of them will never return. These are the mothers who creatively multiply their meager resources so that their children will be clothed and fed, often going hungry themselves and working long hours at various jobs. These are the mothers who would endure any hardship and make any sacrifice for the sake of their families.

Our Christian tradition has many beautiful and exalting teachings about Mary the Mother of Jesus whom we have come to recognize as the Mother of God. From the earliest times, the church has expanded on Mary's own words: "Henceforth all generations will call me blessed." She is the Immaculate Conception, she is the queen of heaven and earth; she is the assumption; she is the tower of ivory, she is the blessed, ever virgin Mother of God, she is the queen of the angels, she is Our Lady of Guadalupe, Our Lady of Lourdes, Our Lady of Fatima, and many other precious titles.

The basis for all these beautiful titles is the reality of Mary the Galilean woman from Nazareth, who probably raised Jesus as a single mother for most of their lives together, witnessed the expulsion of her son by the leaders of her beloved religion ("they handed him over to him [Pilate]" [Mark 15:1]), accompanied him to his cruel execution, and stayed with him till the very end. As a loving mother, she suffered with him all the abuses, misunderstandings, and physical agony.

So it should not be surprising that it is not the lofty titles or elaborate doctrines about Mary that attract the popular devotion of the masses of the faithful but rather her solidarity with us in our suffering. Many of these titles and doctrines emerged out of the popular devotions of the people and were proclaimed precisely to protect them. As the suffering mother, as the one who suffered the scandal of Jesus from conception to death, she can understand us in our suffering, cry with us in our tears, and lament with us in our sorrows. Because suffering of one kind or another is an ordinary element of human life, who better than a suffering mother who did not allow her suffering to destroy her, to give us strength, courage, and hope in our own sufferings and miseries.

It is as if the sense of the faithful intuits what the Church teaches in both Vatican II and the new catechism of the Catholic Church: "This union of the mother with the Son in the work of salvation is made manifest from the time of Christ's virginal conception up to his death. . . . Enduring with her only begotten Son the intensity of his suffering, joining herself with his sacrifice in her mother's heart" (Lumen Gentium 57 and 58, Catechism 964).

The loving union of mother and child became very evident to me one afternoon when I was called to rush to the hospital to minister to a young man dying of AIDS. A car accident had caused a traffic jam on the expressway, and it took me an extra long time to arrive at the hospital. When I finally arrived, the young man was already dead. Sitting by the side of the bed was his mother, whose profound agony was evident in her face and especially her eyes. He was her only son. I thought I was seeing Mary, *the Mater Dolorosa*, at the foot of the cross; her whole body and countenance radiated excruciating pain and resignation, yet there was a fascinating beauty and radiance about her at the same time. I wish I was a painter so that I could have painted that incredible scene so as to give solace and inspiration to others.

I started to say some words of consolation, but it was evident that she was not hearing anything I said; she seemed to be in another world, in a world of innermost silence. Then, as I put my arm around her and just stood there in silence, she began to speak in a very soft but clear voice, a voice coming from the deepest recesses of her heart: "Oh, dear Father, what a wonderful and singular grace God has granted to me on this day. Today I have experienced in my womb what Mary experienced at the death of her son. Mary and I are now united in the death of our sons. What an incredible privilege! With my son, I have tasted the agony of death but now I feel his life within me more than ever before in my life. Praise be God for such a powerful blessing."

It was not I who had brought this courageous woman consolation, but the presence in her consciousness of the sorrowful mother accompanying her son at the moment of his death. This icon, which is present in various forms in all of our Latino Catholic churches, had given her a far richer understanding and appreciation on the salvific and healing power of the various moments of the life of Jesus than any sermon, theological treatise, or explanation could have ever done. This beautiful icon was generative of a terrific illumination. She, like Mary, had contemplated death in her heart, and even though she might not have had any sophisticated explanations, she had grasped the depth of the mysteries of our salvation.

"And you yourself a sword will pierce"—*Luke 2:35*

The gospel according to John presents Mary at the foot of the cross along with a few others, but there is no scriptural reference to Mary tenderly holding the body of her dead son over her lap; yet it is the most striking and consoling icon of our Christian tradition. Even though it is not recorded, I am sure that it took place. Would it not be the very mother who first held him in her arms comfortably resting against her bosom who would now want to hold his body for the last time before taking it for burial? It is said that a picture was worth a thousand words, and I believe that this icon of Mary tenderly holding the body of her son deepens, enriches, and personalizes even our best theological understanding about the suffering of the world more than the best explanations of suffering. We know they are just statues or paintings, yet they are icons—they make the reality represented truly present for those of us who believe.

The *Stabat Mater* ("By the Cross His Mother Standing") is one of the most popular and moving hymns of the Christian tradition and has given rise to great art and musical compositions. One of the most revered works of the great artist Michelangelo is the Pietá, while one of the most popular images and devotions of the Christian world is the Sorrowful Mother, La Dolorosa. There is a profound message in the very presence of the mother in deep sorrow at the foot of the cross and even a deeper one in the body of our savior laying across the lap of his mother. The best of words seem quite empty in expressing what people experience in the presence of La Dolorosa. Out of her womb he came into the world, and into the womb of mother earth she now returns his body.

Chronologically we might say that Jesus entered into the suffering of Mary. She suffered a disturbing fear at the conception of Jesus, and at the end she suffered the horrible execution of her only son. Together, they suffered and sacrificed so that we might have new life. Latin American Christians have a deep appreciation of this salvific bond and enter into it in a very personal way on the evening of Good Friday. The passion of Jesus does not end with the crucifixion. Just as the bright spring sun begins to set over the cities and towns where Latin Americans live, the people gather silently to take the corpse down from the cross. After the massive commotions of the day, a soft and soothing peacefulness quietly permeates throughout the crowds gathered for the *Pésame* (condolences) and *Santo Entierro* (holy burial). It is as if everyone is intimately inter- connected to one another through the astonishment of the events that have just taken place. The many are truly "one in sorrow" at this moment. Yet in spite of the incredible togetherness, it is as if each one is equally totally alone—alone together—in their own deepest sorrow, in their own deepest tragedy, in their own deepest humiliation. It is truly an assembly in solitude, *un pueblo en soledad*. It is the silence of awe, the silence of shock, the silence of astonishment, the silence of unbelief at what has taken place, yet it is equally the silence of profound expectation and anticipation. It is the silence of the unknown, the silence that was probably there at the final moments of the chaos right before creation. The very togetherness of the people of all ages and backgrounds, bonded in sorrowful silence, is itself a loud proclamation of what has just taken place: the dramatic end to an even more dramatic beginning, which already started to burst forth with the innocent victim who shed his blood for us on the cross.

His physical body is certainly dead, but he seems to be more present among us than ever. It is as if the words of the gospel story become present in us: "He handed over the spirit" (John 19:30). We certainly feel this spirit; in fact, we can almost see it and touch it. There is no doubt that the spirit given from the cross is among us now.

The burial procession of Viernes Santo begins with the sorrowful mother following closely behind the body of her son. As we walk with the mother in grief and the body of her dead son, we ponder the life and mysteries of this courageous woman who never gave up. What is the mystery of this very special barrio woman that continues to give courage, strength, and life to the suffering of the world? In her life, she never appeared to be anything special. She was very much like our own hardworking mothers who sacrifice themselves without reserve for the welfare of their families. Through her wrinkled face and calloused hands, she radiates the beauty of a dedicated life. She is bent over from the harsh work of cooking, laundry, and cleaning. Her face is a beautiful expression of sorrow but not of resentment, anger, or disgust. She was not a temple virgin, queen, actress, singer, writer, or wonderwoman of any sort. Yet, as the sorrowful mother of the crucified, she has become the most revered and most beautiful of any woman, of any human being in the world. She would not have won any beauty contest or appeared in any beauty magazine, yet she is easily recognized by millions around the world and throughout the centuries as the most beautiful woman in the world. She probably looked much more like a elderly working mother than a media icon.

What incredible strength and beauty come through every fiber of this frail woman's aging body with the white hair and sun-drenched skin of a life of hard work, tears, trials, and tribulations. It is the strength which has enabled our mothers and our fathers—the mothers and fathers of the poor—to endure hardship, insult, ridicule, hunger, fatigue, loneliness, and even prostitution for the sake of their beloved children. The crucified peoples of the world understand well the holding-strength and saving power of this apparently frail and helpless woman. She does not approve of or legitimize the injustices that bring this suffering about, but neither does she allow them to destroy her, diminish her dignity, or squash her love and confidence in her son.

As the birth of God passed through the birth pains of Mary, so now the birth of the new people of God, the faithful followers of Jesus, will pass through the death pains of the sorrowful mother—*La Soledad*. Alone, she received the news of her unexpected and unusual pregnancy, alone with Joseph she gave birth to her son and then immigrated into Egypt, alone she raised her son, and alone with only a few friends she saw him condemned and die on the cross. Jesus suffered as a man, and Mary suffered as a woman what no man could have suffered. Thus, together they rehabilitate humanity; together they are the coredeemers of humanity. Her very silent solitude is the womb that gives birth to the new fellowship of men and women, people brought into a totally new life through the life, death, and resurrection of Jesus.

"Behold, your mother"—*John 19:27*

In her suffering Mary becomes the universal mother because there is no parent who cannot identify with her. She, like all parents, is the mother who suffers in the deepest recesses of her being the fate of her children. Yet every parent can equally gain strength from her, for her inner strength did not allow the most devastating humiliation to humiliate her, shatter her composure, destroy her dignity, or rattle her mental well-being. Sorrows could not destroy her life, and in her very sorrows, La Soledad gives life to the sorrowful who come to her—and she is always there for us.

But the sorrowful mother is equally there for all of us, her children who are often misunderstood by others, even our own human parents. She is here for children, her adult and aging children, who like all children, make mistakes, fall, get bruised, and need consolation. Here is the compassionate mother who always understands, who always receives me, who can always console me with the tenderness of her arms, her bosom, and her hands. When I am pushed away by everyone, physically and emotionally, it is good to have someone I can come to who will absorb my sorrows into her own.

I learned this well as a young child; my grandmother would tell and retell us the story of how the sorrowful mother had come to her rescue. My grandmother was very young when her husband died unexpectedly. It was a time of great turmoil in Mexico City. My grandmother was left penniless with a young family and household to support. She was about to lose everything. In desperation, she went to the cathedral to pray to the Sorrowful Mother, who would certainly understand her. In every church in Mexico you will find a statue of La Dolorosa, the Madonna all dressed in black and evidently in great sorrow. When she returned home, the person who was taking care of the children handed her an envelope and told her that while she was away, a lady dressed in black had come to deliver this envelope to her. The envelope had enough money to carry them through until my grandmother could get a job. The way the lady was described to my grandmother, there was no doubt in my grandmother's mind that it was La Dolorosa who had come to answer her prayer precisely at the moment she was praying to her. She is truly the compassionate mother who comes to our aid in moments of need or even just to be with us in our moments of great sorrow. She can understand; she has been there!

"And from that hour the disciple took her to his own home"—*John 19:27*

As the burial procession on Good Friday comes to an end around the main plaza of San Antonio and people have exchanged personal experiences of suffering with the sorrowful mother, the people gradually walk by the corpse to pay their final respects and leave a flower upon the body that even in death continues to give life to us. In these moments of intense sharing—at this moment so private and so public, so personal and so general at the same time—the peace of the Lord, the peace that the world can never give, begins to invade our hearts and soothes the entire congregation. Words of comfort are no longer needed, for the peace of Christ truly permeates our entire being; words of explanation become quite secondary, for the insights of this entire day will illuminate and guide our lives in a new path. It seems that as we place the simple flower over Jesus' body, given for our salvation, we receive the first spark of his own life within us. It is an experience beyond words to describe but easily evident in the faces of the people as they walk by, young and old, to pay their final respects. We truly begin to feel the peace that the risen Lord offered to the disciples in the cenacle after his resurrection. Maybe if they had not run out and hidden, they, too, might have received that peace even as they were burying the body of Jesus.

As the people leave the church in San Antonio on Good Friday, it is as if the words of the final Marian hymn confirm and motivate the new life they have experienced: "Aunque te digan algunos que nada puede cambiar, lucha por un mundo Nuevo y otros te seguirán" ("Even though some people will say that nothing can change, struggle for a new world, and others will follow you"). Now, we must carry on the work of Jesus in the world, no matter the cost, no matter the sacrifice. He did it for us; we must do it for others. But we will never be alone, because his mother will be right there with us, giving us all the strength and courage we need to overcome any obstacle and plough through any difficulty as we continue to work for the construction of the new creation.

The people have taken the Lord's final gift to heart. The loving, compassionate, and sacrificing Mother of Jesus has become our mother. She will be with us in our lives, our homes, and all our struggles. It is as if the words of Our Lady of Guadalupe to Juan Diego were already spoken to us in the final gift of Jesus from the cross: "You have nothing to fear; am I not here who am your mother?" And who knows, maybe the beloved disciple and all the others did experience these very words in the postresurrection presence of Mary among them (Acts 1:14).

~

CHAPTER ELEVEN

A New Humanity

**"Blessed are you who are poor,
for the kingdom of God is yours"**—*Luke 6:20*

People who believe in Jesus Christ experience nothing less than a real rebirth of mind and heart. The world has not changed, but they are totally changed. Through them, more human social structures will emerge and begin to take shape. They continue to be in the world struggling with the same daily affairs as anyone else, yet they are no longer of the world. They continue to live and struggle in the world like anyone else, yet they rise above the ordinary enslaving and destructive attitudes of sinful society. They are in the world, but beyond it. Many continue to live a crucified existence, yet they have already risen from the dead; many continue to be poor, destitute, and disenfranchised, yet they are rich beyond all the material wealth of this world; many are still illiterate, yet they have a wisdom far greater than the many intellectuals. They might still be marginal within society, yet they are the dynamic center of a new humanity like the world has never known.

This newness of life of the early Christian communities has become very evident to me in working with the Christian poor in various parts of the world. The wounds of their crucified lives are certainly apparent in their small bodies, wrinkled faces, calloused hands, missing teeth, poor clothing, old scars of illness or childhood burns, and other deformities caused by prolonged hunger and disease, yet the joy of divine life shines through their eyes like brilliant sunrays and resonates through their songs like a heavenly chorus. They are the continuation of the very first poor and dispossessed who found new life in the following of Jesus.

A few years ago I participated in the annual summer school for leaders of the *Comunidades de Base* in Lima, Peru. Several thousand people had gathered for the annual two-week course. Some had traveled two or three days by bus to get there. Others brought their young daughters to babysit while the mothers took part in the courses. The topic for this year was "The God of Life." It was amazing that the poor who were robbed of life in so many ways were exploring and celebrating the God of life!

A few months later, I attended a symposium of Nordic European university students on "the right to choose one's way and the moment of death." It was startling! Those who had everything were concerned with dying, while those who had nothing were concerned with life! *¡Qué locura!*

The participants in Lima's summer program were from among the poorest of the poor of the region. Extreme poverty and misery have deprived the masses of Latin America and the Caribbean of the most basic necessities of life. One could easily say that they are born and live in the valley of death. Their faces were wrinkled from working in the outdoors, it was evident they had not had any constructive dental work, and many looked much older than their actual age. No cosmetics to hide the reality of their being! They slept in the outdoors, ate the most simple foods, had no comforts whatsoever, and yet were the happiest people I have ever met. Throughout the corridors there was laughter, people easily broke out into song before the sessions, and all presentations were peppered with a lot of good humor.

The closing liturgy is an event I will never forget. There was nothing fancy or elegant about the hall turned into worship space, but the spirit of the people quickly transformed it into the most beautiful and vibrant cathedral I have ever visited. No one was dressed with fancy clothing or adorned with exquisite jewels, but the brightness of their eyes and the beauty of their countenances were astounding. They were like living diamonds radiating beautiful lights. It was as if an inner light had been turned on within each one of them and together they illuminated the entire hall with a sort of supernatural light. The joy that permeated the entire celebration was contagious.

There was no great choir with a well-rehearsed choral, but the simple instruments of the people and the joy-filled voices of the entire assembly made the most powerful and beautiful church music I have ever experienced. There were no elegant vestments or high church rituals, just the simple entrance of the celebrant accompanied by the various ministers dressed in the ordinary clothing of the people. The utter humble simplicity of the celebrant and congregation gave it a majesty I have never experienced in any papal liturgy or anywhere else. This was truly a community of life!

In hindsight I remembered that I had experienced something similar in the celebrations of the *Cursillo* movement and later on would work to bring about similar celebrations in San Fernando Cathedral, the cathedral especially of the poor and marginal of San Antonio. In prayerful reflection I realized that what I was experiencing in these groups was the living tradition of Christianity that had begun with the very first followers of Christ. This was not the historical tradition that one studies and reads about in books, but the very reality of the living tradition that is the life source of Christianity. It was the new life of the marginal and "nothings" of the world that had attracted peoples of all walks of life, of all ethnicities, and of various religions to join those who, in the power of the spirit, now lived according to "the way" of Jesus. The marginal had not been transformed into the powerful of society, but they had now discovered a new center of belonging, a new status, and a new power that relativized everything else in this world.

We tend to look at the life, crucifixion, resurrection of Christ, and the reception of the Spirit at Pentecost in a quick and simple confessional way but fail to appreciate the incredible transforming power of those who first experienced these events and subsequently of those who experienced them through the witness and preaching of the followers of Jesus. Christ did not just rise from the dead; he has risen in his followers to such an extent that every believer can say of himself the words of Paul: "I live, no longer I, but Christ lives in me" (Galatians 2:20).

"We were hoping that he would be the one to redeem Israel"—*Luke 24:21*

All his enemies and friends thought Jesus was completely and disgracefully finished. Crucified, dead, buried, and gone forever! Just as when he was born in the silence of the night and away from the city in borrowed space, the totally unimagined surprise now took place. Jesus came forth from the dead like a spark that would ignite a new fire of love, like a flare that would illuminate the darkness of hearts and minds, like an energy that would empower others to love as he had loved. In hindsight, the resurrection should not be too surprising since the entire life of Jesus was a series of unsuspected surprises, like the building blocks of the new creation. Now, the project could begin in its fullness. Worldly wisdom had become so confused and even perverted that the ways of a loving God would seem irrational and even blasphemous.

The resurrection of Jesus from the dead comes to its fullness on the first Easter morning. I say this because as I meditate and ponder in my heart the life of Jesus in relation to his culture, religion, and society, it is evident that Jesus was constantly "resurrecting" from the many circumstances that condemn people to various types of social death. He was constantly surprising people in every aspect of his life, actions, and teachings. From the very beginning, Jesus sacrificed for the sake of new breakthroughs in every aspect of life. He was victimized in many ways, but was never destroyed. He rose above the forces of insults, prejudice, malice, segregation, hypocrisy, and injustice and not only lived the dignified life of a truly free man but invited others into the same life, to become children of the same Father! This is the incredible power of living in intimate union with God.

The ultimate sacrifice of Jesus for the sake of the salvation of humanity was certainly his death on the cross. But that was not the only sacrifice. In fact, it was the culmination of an entire life of sacrifices for the sake of liberating us from the shackles of sin by revealing, in his very flesh and blood, the truth of men and women and the truth of God.

Jesus was a man of great sacrifices and incredible suffering, yet he was not a sad and mournful person. He would not allow his victimizers to destroy him, for his love remained greater than their offenses. He was not a prophet of doom but a herald of festive joy. No wonder the lifeless and depressed crowds were so attracted to him. I wish the gospel stories would have recorded his jokes, for I'm sure he had a great sense of humor; isn't laughter one of the great gifts of God? I also think that he enjoyed singing popular songs; after all, David who was a prototype of Jesus, was the great poet-singer. He was indeed a man of great sacrifices, but he was not a gloomy person. He transcended the gloom of the world and radiated the brightness of God's presence. He rose above the sadness of suffering to celebrate the joy of life.

The time of mourning had elapsed and the time of joy had arrived: "This is the time of fulfillment. The kingdom of God is at hand" (Mark 1:15). In fact, he was known to have good times with the marginal outcasts as well as with the elite of society. He reversed the expectations of society by revealing the God-rooted happiness of the poor, the hungry, the mournful, the pure of heart, the merciful, the peacemakers, the justice seekers, and even the persecuted

(Matthew 5:1–11). Salvation was not in the damnation of anyone, but in the feast of everyone beginning with the marginal and disenfranchised of society and religion.

Jesus sacrificed a respectable social status by being a marginal Galilean Jew. He sacrificed the social legitimacy of his life by being conceived of an unwed mother. He sacrificed the comfort and security of a home by being born among the homeless. He sacrificed his reputation by mixing freely with anyone, especially the social and religious outcasts of his time. He sacrificed his love of a woman and a family for the sake of loving everyone. He sacrificed his life by refusing to give in to the violent ways of society. They were the sacrifices of a lover for the sake of the beloved. Greater beauty than this does not exist!

Indeed Jesus was a man of sacrifice, and redeemed humanity has intuited perfectly the beauty of the sacrifices by exalting the various moments of the sacrifice in the most beautiful ways possible—conception, birth, and death. His most vulnerable moments are today's most cherished symbols. The annunciation, the birth among the homeless shepherds, various incidents of his life, and most especially his passion, crowning with thorns, flagellation, and crucifixion have inspired the most beautiful and moving works of art and music throughout the centuries and throughout the continents.

Yet his life did not end in suffering and sacrifice but in unexpected joy. The one whom the world had rejected and executed, God raised gloriously from the dead. In the resurrection, God proclaims the divine approval of the way of Jesus. What had appeared as scandalous, blasphemous, and even diabolical to some would now become the way of true life and holiness. What had appeared as the abandonment of God and even a curse from God (Deuteronomy 21:23, Galatians 3:13) would now be seen and appreciated in a totally new way. He was not a God who abandoned his son in his hour of supreme need, or a God who subjected his son to horrible punishment, but a God who empowered his son to break the shackles of evil not by introducing a greater evil but through the power of love and love alone. No matter the cost, this was the only way to break the power of evil to generate even greater evil. God did not curse his son, but rather blessed humanity through the divine love re-leased into the world by his son. This indeed was creative of spon-taneous joy, as when an insignificant team triumphs over the cham-pions in the final moments of a ball game to walk away with the coveted trophy. The spontaneous joy, cheers, dances, and celebra-tions of their supporters do not have to be programmed or orches-trated by anyone. The spirit of triumph permeates their whole selves and is evident through every motion of their bodies and sounds from their mouths. This was the spontaneous hymns of joy composed by the first Christians (Acts 16:25, Ephesians 5:19, Colossians 3:16). The one in whom they had hoped had not been defeated. He had won! He had won in a totally unsuspected way. He had been killed, but God had raised him! Alleluia!

"Peace be with you"—*John 20:19*

The very first act of the risen Lord was to go visit his close friends who had run out on him on Friday when he needed them the most. Would he scold them for being cowards? Would he tell them how totally disappointed he was in them? Would he question them as to why they had run out on him? Would he call them weaklings and traitors? They certainly deserved it. Yet the only words he said to them were: "Peace be with you!" (John 20:19).

I think we can very legitimately reconstruct the moment. The disciples were gathered and still in great shock and fear. At the sight of the Lord I am sure there was a combination of joy and shame—joy because he was alive, shame because they had abandoned him. How could they ever face him, look him in the eyes when they had betrayed him? I am sure Peter was having nightmares remembering the eye-to-eye contact with Jesus at the very moment he was deny-ing him because of the remarks of a young girl (Luke 22:61). Yet, in the very look of the eyes of Jesus, they saw not anger, reproach, or disappointment, but tenderness, love, and welcome. The radical forgiveness that had been a hallmark of his life and ministry is now offered to them. Not because they had been correct in what they had done, not because it had not hurt him to be abandoned in his hour of greatest need, but because God's love is greater than the offense. Jesus came to rehabilitate through love and not to condemn through righteousness. The wounds are still there and the pain is still there, but the poison of revenge or other demands for retaliation is dissolved by the forgiveness of love.

The bonds of friendship and fellowship ruptured by the betrayal are now reestablished and become even stronger. They had seen Jesus forgive others, but now it was they, his closest friends (and no one can hurt and disappoint you more than the ones you love the most), who experienced his unlimited and even undeserving loving forgiveness. Given the cultural and religious values of the times and even today, this must have been a totally unsuspected experience. He was offering forgiveness not because they had recognized their sin and shown remorse, not because he was too weak to take revenge of some sort or another, but because his love was more powerful than ever.

I suspect that in this experience they came to a far deeper appreciation of forgiveness and reconciliation than they had ever imagined. They began to experience in their own flesh and blood the forgiveness Jesus had been practicing all along.

Having regrouped his friends into a community of forgiveness, Jesus spent some time with them in one of his favorite activities, table fellowship, and in giving them some final instructions before ascending into heaven. Shortly after, on Pentecost morning, he sent the Spirit to them, just like he had promised. It was like a volcanic irruption of spiritual energy! It was like the first creative force that brought order out of the chaos (Genesis 1) but in many ways much more marvelous, for radically new human beings would be created out of the old. As God had breathed into the nostrils of Adam to give him life (Genesis 2:7), so now Christ breathed into the "old humans" so as to bring them to new life (John 20:22). Vengeful and destructive human beings would now be forgiving human beings, creators of a new human community of love.

"Are not all these people who are speaking Galileans?"—Acts 2:7

On Pentecost, all of a sudden, the Galileans who had previously been difficult to understand because of their heavy accent now spoke in a way that everyone understood. The same Galileans, who had been paralyzed by fear, now go out fearlessly into the open spaces to confess that Jesus, who had been crucified, was risen and the Lord of salvation! The Galileans, who had had nothing of value to offer, now had the best and most life-giving thing to offer! Indeed, "The stones rejected by the builders" (Matthew 21:42, Mark 12:10–11, Luke 20: 17–18) were now becoming the foundation stones of the new humanity. Empires would not be overthrown, but a new force would invade them in totally unsuspected ways. Kingdoms would not overtake one another, but a new reign of universal love would spread its power to all kingdoms. Empires and kingdoms would not be conquered, but the minds and hearts of people would be captivated by the new family of God to which they now belonged.

What was this new force that would conquer not earthly kingdoms but the hearts and minds of men and women anywhere? It was the power of the risen Lord now present in the community of his followers. Christ had not only risen from the dead, he had arisen within the lives of his followers. They are totally re-created so that they could easily say as St. Paul said: "I live, no longer I, but Christ lives in me" (Galatians 2:20). This new group did not go off in hiding to form some kind of sect of the "elect" but rather lived out their lives in such a new way that others of all classes, religions, and ethnicities were attracted to "the way." Even at the cost of great sacrifices, many wanted to become part of this new group that could no longer be classified according to any of the world's categories of classification, for it was inclusive of everyone without exception. No wonder people began to speak about the early Christians as "the third race." Previous boundaries of separation had no power over the new force of unity that was emerging and quickly spreading. Titles of nobility and priesthood became quite relative in relation to the newfound title for all who joined the new group: brother and sister. If God is truly our father, then we, regardless of how the world looks upon us, are brothers and sisters. As Jesus had reversed many of the notions and customs of his time, he reversed even the image and meaning of "father" from that of an authoritarian, dominating, and controlling patriarch to that of the merciful father who unites the new family through tenderness, compassion, forgiveness, and love. He likewise changes the hierarchical image and meaning of "family" to one of loving and caring equality where neither sex, nor age, nor wordly status will make any difference.

This was no complicated or esoteric mystery religion. In fact, it was its simplicity that attracted so many followers, a simplicity in recognizing the true value of life and rejoicing in the newly discovered fellowship. It was so simple and so human that religious people of that time considered them atheists. The Christians might not have many of the world's goods, they might not have any noble titles, and they might not appear important to the world; but what did any of that matter for they now had the greatest treasure of all: the intimate parenthood of a loving and caring God lived out in the new fellowship of prayer, study, concern for one another, and the celebration of "the breaking of the bread" (Acts 2:42). But this was no exclusive fellowship. From the very beginning, it was open to all! Your identity or status or even your past did not matter. It was not important whether you were pure or impure, local or foreigner, rich or poor, Jew or Gentile, man or woman, free or enslaved, priest or layperson, intellectual or illiterate; you were welcomed and desired! What mattered was your acceptance of the Lord in your life.

The joy that this new mixed community experienced was so great that it broke into spontaneous songs of praise and thanksgiving. I am sure that even when strangers could not understand what they were talking about, they understood the deeper language of joy and *agape*. This became very evident to me when we started projecting the San Fernando Mass to the entire United States. At that time, the Mass was in Spanish, as it was mainly intended for the Spanish speakers who often did not have services in Spanish in their local church. Almost immediately, we started to have participants who did not know Spanish. Not a single one asked us to change to English, but we did get beautiful notes basically saying the same thing: "We don't understand what you are saying, but it is not really important because the service is so beautiful and joyful that we know we are in the presence of God." Many would travel to San Antonio just to attend Mass at San Fernando. One elderly Irish woman wrote: "As I am quite old, I think of death a lot. If Heaven is going to be anything like your Masses, I can't wait to get there." People who did come to San Fernando often expressed the beautiful welcome and concern they experienced by being there. This was the transforming force of the early Christian community! Never overpowering anyone, but attracting them through the joy that is the expression of the fellowship of love.

"Come, Lord Jesus"—*Revelation 22:20*

There is no doubt that we as Christians look forward to the final coming of Christ in all his glory at the end of time. But in the meantime, Christ has not abandoned us and left us alone. He is very much present among us, especially among the Galileans of today's world, that is, the poor, the marginal, and the disinherited of society. In the cries and struggles of the poor and the marginalized, we know that the work of Christ in building the reign of God is not yet complete. In the very struggles of their suffering, we hear the urgent cry: "Come Lord Jesus!" And we know that he will not only come at the end of time, but he comes to us today.

Christ is very much present in the struggles of the farmworkers for just wages and decent working conditions. Christ is present in the community organizing struggles for justice in our American society. Christ is present in the struggles of everyone who is working to better humanity. The same transforming spirit that was experienced by the first Christians at Pentecost is present today in the communities and celebrations of the Christian poor struggling for survival and for justice. I have experienced this spirit in many communities of the Christian poor around the world, as many missionaries can equally attest to. But I have also experienced this in my own city of San Antonio where many modern-day Galileans make their home.

CHAPTER TWELVE

~

If Jesus Had Lived in San Antonio

"Then Jesus said to them, 'Do not
be afraid. Go tell my brothers to go to
Galilee, and there they will see me.'"—*Matthew 28:10*

Can you imagine seeing Jesus today? Jesus certainly did not mean
that disciples of the following generations would have to go physically to Galilee in order to see him, but I am sure he meant that in
order to see and know him well, in order to truly understand what
he was about, we had to know his entire life as lived between
Galilee and Jerusalem. The beautifully redemptive force of his actions and words emerge clearly and powerfully in the context of the
cultural and social reality of his times. The impoverished and colonized periphery of Galilee became the new center of divine inter-
vention, and a simple charismatic peasant emerges as the firstborn
and herald of the new humanity.

So, do you want to see, understand, and appreciate Jesus today? I
cannot think of a better way than to enter into the lives of those
who are living similar experiences and struggles today, those living
in the "Galilees" of today's world, those living in the margins and

crossroads of civilizations. They will have perspectives into the actions and words of Jesus that textual studies alone, especially when done out of totally different contexts, will not even suspect. The very cultural experiences of the people become a powerful lens through which to read the Gospels and serve as parables for an understanding of the Gospels. When the Gospels are read this way, they in turn become the interpretive lens through which our own life and struggles take on a beautiful new meaning and direction.

As I read the many excellent studies on Galilee, the land where Jesus was raised and carried on most of his ministry, I feel that if he had lived today, he could have lived in a region like San Antonio, Texas, or better yet, in one of the small surrounding towns such as Stockdale, Floresville, Las Gallinas, Panna Maria, or Elmendorff. Cafarnaum would be to San Antonio what Nazareth would be to one of the small rural towns. I think Jesus could have easily lived in the carpentry shop close to where we lived in one of the Mexican barrios of San Antonio.

Galilean Texas

The situation of the Mexican-American people in Texas and the southwest of the United States has been very similar to that of the Jews in Palestine. At the time of Jesus, Galilee was a colony of the Roman Empire that had adopted many of the features of the predominant Greek culture, which itself was a combination of the cultures of the East and the West. Through the cultural mixing efforts of Alexander the Great, Greek culture had not only dominated and influenced much of the known world of that time, and especially Palestine, but incorporated many of the features of the very peoples he had conquered. Yet previous conquests by the Babylonian and Persian empires had also left their cultural influence in the land of Jesus. Conscious or unconscious cultural exchange had been taking place in many ways. Like the Jews, the native and Mexican-American people of Texas have experienced various invasions and forms of foreign domination. They had been conquered and colonized first by Spain, then Mexico, then the Republic of Texas, then the United States and even the Confederacy of the South. Like the Jews of Palestine, they had been dominated and influenced by the various people who had come by and installed themselves in this land.

Jesus could have been a Mexican-American carpenter living and working in Texas, formerly a part of Mexico and now what some refer to as "an internal colony of the United States." He may not have been the poorest of the poor, but perhaps one of the rather poor, marginal, and insignificant people on the edges of mainstream society. His first language would have been Spanish instead of Aramaic. He would have spoken mispronounced English—perhaps the mixture of Spanish and English we call "Tex-Mex"—rather than mispronounced Greek. He would have gone through substandard schools, leaving him ineligible for higher education or seminary studies. Instead of the synagogue, his Mexican parish church would have been the place where he would have hung around to celebrate all the feasts of his people and to learn about his God and the traditions of many of his people.

Much like the Galilean Jews, the Mexican people of the area might be poor and under the power of a larger government, landowners, and business, but they have never lost their sense of dignity, pride, and most of all their faith. An unquestioned faith and confidence in "la Divina Providencia," expressed through Jesus Nazareno and Nuestra Señora de Guadalupe, has enabled the Mexican people of Texas to withstand whatever hardships came their way without being broken in spirit or disillusioned with life. They've suffered many insults and abuses, but have never lost their love of life and fiesta. In fact, it is the religious-cultural fiestas that have kept the people strong, together, and alive. It is this unquestioned faith that has given the Mexican-American poor hope against all human hope that God will triumph and things will get better. "*Esperemos en Dios*" ("let us hope in God") is a very common expression among the people; it's a common way of saying "Come

Lord Jesus." This isn't an expression of fatalism, as some outside scholars have claimed, but a complete trust that the justice of God will uplift the downtrodden and right the wrongs of society. It is this hope in the apparently useless struggle that has not only kept the people alive, but been the very basis of the joy that is experienced in the fiestas of the people.

Jesus grew up in a small town where life was centered around the local synagogue in what seems to have been a very religious Jewish family. Likewise, in the "*religión casera*" of our homes, the basic prayers, blessing, and tenants of the faith are learned at home while the local Mexican Catholic parish is the center of our social and religious life. It is the one place we can be ourselves without having to be afraid or apologetic about who we are. An occasional pilgrimage to Jerusalem and the Temple was the dream and highlight of the Jewish people in Galilee, just as a lifetime pilgrimage to Tepeyac is the dream of all our people.

Jesus does not seem to have had any formal education but was imbued with a deep love for his Jewish tradition. He learned the simple essentials of his faith from his parents and relatives. I am sure that as in many small Mexican towns, in Nazareth almost everyone was related to each other in one way or another. He probably did not know the theological intricacies of his religion as expounded by the learned doctors of the faith, but he was filled with the small-town theological wisdom of those who have pondered the meaning of their faith tradition in their hearts and tried to live it in their everyday lives. He probably was not acquainted with any of the liturgical rituals of the Temple, but he knew, loved, and practiced the popular religious devotions of his people. He had learned the Scriptures well not by studying them formally with the learned scholars, but by hearing about them in the regular synagogue practice from the ordinary people of the land—the very people who were often considered to be pubic sinners because of their ignorance of the details of the law and their frequent contact with pagans. This is the way many of our people have learned the basics of our Catholic faith and transmitted to it others, yet our practices and devotions are often misunderstood and even ridiculed by some experts on religion.

There is no doubt that Jesus was very Jewish, yet at the same time he could not escape being deeply influenced by the other ethnicities that likewise lived in that region, most of all the Greek culture of that time. Hellenism was looked upon by many, especially some aristocratic Jews, as a superior culture. Anyone who wanted to better themselves would seek to assimilate the Greek way of life—even to the extent of disguising their circumcision. They strived to become Hellenized while remaining Jews in some sort of flimsy fashion. A similar desire to "Americanize" is strong among the wealth-aristocracy of Mexico, who often ridicule the efforts of Mexican-Americans to maintain with pride the cultural heritage of Mexico while adjusting to life in the United States.

In Galilee people strived to maintain a purity of their Jewish ways, but it was not possible to stand off the intrusion of other cultures. Whether one wanted to become Hellenized or not, just by living in that region of the world at that particular time, some elements of Greek culture became part of the being and thought of the Jewish community. We have certainly experienced this in Texas—no matter how Mexican one wants to remain, U.S.-Anglo culture penetrates our souls and becomes part of our being. We have not ceased being Mexican, but gradually we've become Americanized, our very being is an evolving synthesis. Yet as such, we've been distanced from both Mexicans and Anglo-Americans. Both have looked down on us as impure and contaminated, ridiculed our speech, and considered us to be inferior to them.

The oppression of the colonized Mexican people of Texas has been holistic. No aspect of our lives has been left untouched or unscarred. The oppression was not only economic (since they had replaced the slaves after the elimination of slavery in the South) but also linguistic, cultural, and religious. Schooling had been substandard so as to keep the people ignorant, the mestizo culture had been stereotyped by the dominant culture as inferior and incapable, the Spanish language of the area had been deemed as a sign of backwardness, and our mestizo Catholic practices have been considered as pagan and superstitious by both Protestant and Catholic clergy alike. I suspect that this was very much the way that the experts of religion looked upon the Galilean practices, especially around the Temple.

Yet, like the Jews of Galilee, the Mexican people of Texas have maintained a deep sense of identity, pride, and sense of gratitude to God for being who we are. As my grandmother used to say when she would hear ugly remarks about our people: "Pray that God may illuminate them; they are so ignorant of the truth." There was a deep pain and sometimes even a sense of shame that touched the depths of the soul, but always a sense that God would triumph on our behalf.

I was born and raised in one of the new *colonias* of San Antonio on the outskirts of the city. Ever since the treaty of Guadalupe-Hidalgo whereby 50 percent of Mexico was taken over by the United States, the Mexican people living in the Southwest have been like an internal colony of the United States. Like the Jews of Galilee, we lived under a colonial government and were treated as a colonized people—foreigners in our own land. Yet, like the Jews of Galilee, we have remained proud of our language and heritage and have continued to live and celebrate it. But as we looked at the conditions of poverty in Mexico and the lack of opportunities for advancement for the peons and the poor of Mexico, we were very happy to be in the United States. I suspect Joseph felt pretty much the same way about living in Galilee—it was a much better land, and living far from the center of power had its advantages.

My father was a very proud Mexican-American, yet he was very happy to live in the United States and truly admired many of its ways, though he was critical of others. He saw the United States as the land of freedom and opportunity, yet many of its people appeared arrogant and prejudiced. He would joke about it, saying, "Well, some of our own people are even worse!" He used to say, "If I lived in Mexico, I would be a peon answering to some harsh patrón. Here I am free to be my own boss!" His greatest satisfaction was that he was his own boss.

I grew up in a neighborhood of Mexican-American old-timers and immigrants who were all hardworking simple people of great wisdom and integrity. Some of the old-timers would often remark: "We did not cross the border; the border crossed us!" I can still remember the fascinating philosophical discussions that the men held in the backyard of our store while the women did their shopping. Everyone was very Mexican but very happy to be living in the United States where they could create their own businesses and be their own boss! They had come out of a land of peasants and tyrannical patrones to create a new society where they would enjoy dignity and freedom. The parish church, like the synagogue in the Jewish towns of Galilee, was our social and religious center of life. We loved and cherished our Mexican-mestizo Catholic tradition with its many colorful ceremonies, processions, pilgrimages, shrines, songs, devotions, and decorations. Church was never dull, for even the snoring old folks provided some good entertainment during the services. A pilgrimage to Tepeyac to visit Our Lady of Guadalupe at least once in a lifetime was a must! I'll never forget my first pilgrimage, probably at about the same age that Jesus made the pilgrimage to Jerusalem. It was like going into the very womb of the origins of our people and experiencing the connection, not just with one another but with previous generations and generations to come, and even more so with the entire cosmos! No one had to explain it to us, but we definitely experienced it. From parish church experience to Tepeyac, from local synagogue to the Jerusalem Temple, religion is the very basis of the being and the identity of both the Galileans and the Mexicans. We are poor by society's standards and considered inferior by much of the mainline society, but our religion provides us with a sacred space where we can experience a deep sense of dignity, identity, and belonging.

When I was growing up in San Antonio, racial divisions were rigid and legally enforced. Blacks were kept out or apart without question. But other ethnic divisions were also well marked in San Antonio, as throughout the country. Mexicans were not allowed in some swimming pools except on Wednesday when the pool would be cleaned after closing. Many restaurants refused us services, non-Mexican Catholic churches chased us out and told us to go to the Mexican Church, and schools tried to convince us that we did not have what it took to get through college. If racial and ethnic divisions were the order of the day, so were religious ones. Those were the days before ecumenism, and religion was another powerful barrier that kept people apart. We wouldn't dare go into each other's churches! Racial, ethnic, religious, class, and gender segregation was accepted as God's way for humanity.

Yet in our neighborhood, and especially in my Dad's grocery store, things were completely different; I suspect they were very much they way they would have been in Joseph's carpentry shop and in other small establishments of Galilee. Blacks, Jews, poor Baptist and Methodist whites, and of course Mexicans came by the store to shop and to make friends. I grew up with friends of various races, ethnicities, and religions. Everyone loved being who they were, and they all had the best jokes to tell about their own race or ethnicity and even more so about their churches! Everyone was faithful to their church or synagogue, yet they all poked fun at their own ministers and religious traditions. Sometimes there even seemed to be a contest as to whose religion was the funniest and most crazy! It was great fun. Yet never was the faith of any one of us challenged or questioned. We had a deep respect for everyone, and that is why we could joke so easily together.

The good-natured joking was a simple but profound way of affirming with gratitude and pride what each one of us was, while at the same time recognizing that God was greater and beyond our limitations. It kept all of us from making idols of our own religious tradition. None of us questioned the truth of the tenants of our own faith, but through our friendships and humor, we constantly enriched each other with our differences. It would have been quite dull and boring if there had been no differences.

From our black friends, I started to admire the expressive nature of the Pentecostal experience. From our Jewish friends, I developed a great love for the prophets of the Old Testament and how their faith had enabled them to survive various persecutions. From our Protestant white friends I learned the love for the Bible and of great preaching. Often, they would comment how much they loved our Catholic rituals. Through all this, my Catholic faith was not weakened, but rather expanded! Could you not imagine Jesus being part of this group, asking questions of everyone and joining in both the wisdom and the laughter of the group?

While the rest of society was building barriers of segregation, my Dad's store was, as I see it today, very much like the table fellowship of Jesus in Galilee: Everyone was welcomed and appreciated. The usual segregating and dehumanizing boundaries of society were easily transgressed without any particular scandal to anyone—except the local priest and Protestant minister, who thought people from their congregations should not be hanging around with each other. But that did not bother any one of us too much. In having a good time together, the boundaries of separation were dissolved and the true beauty of everyone present came through. White doctors, Jewish merchants, and Mexican workers could enjoy a beer and good conversation together without any hesitation. The older I get, the more I appreciate these early formative experiences, which showed me the great potential there is in bringing diverse peoples together, not to make them the same but to combine the differences in an enriching way. Each one has much to offer and much to receive. In our very differences, when we come together in the fellowship of friendship, the new creation begins to emerge. I often wonder if Jesus had similar thoughts as he was growing up in Galilee. In God's providence, this was a great preparation for his inauguration of the new humanity of the reign of God.

Redemption: *Viva la Causa*

Jesus was a fervent Jew in Galilee of the Gentiles at a time when Judaism was undergoing a reawakening in pride and fervor. Very much like the early days of the Mexican-American movement in the United

States of the 1960s and the 1970s, there was a Jewish quest in Galilee to "return to the origins. . . . To return to our lost Paradise." Much like the Mexican-Americans living in the United States, the Galilean Jews were struggling to retain, redefine, and celebrate their Jewish identity in the context of the growing and penetrating influence of the dominant Greco-Roman world. No matter how much our people would have wanted to remain "purely Mexican," they could not prevent the influence of Anglo culture any more than the Jews of Galilee could keep from becoming Hellenized. This is happening today in the Americanization of the whole world; whether nations want it or not, it is happening. Yet, do ethnicities have to be trampled upon or die for people to become part of the emerging global community?

In the Palestine of Jesus, redemption was in the air! God would bring forth the Messiah and liberate the Jewish people from the oppressive powers. We experienced a similar movement after the end of World War II. Charismatic leaders started to emerge throughout the Southwest. For some, our liberation would come in the complete restoration of Aztlan, the mythical land of our origins, sort of like the Jewish quest for the restoration of the Davidic kingdom.

In the beginning of this liberation movement, it seemed like everything "gringo" was evil and contaminated. Some felt that we had to purify ourselves of all the contaminating influences of the United States. At the opposite end of the struggles, others felt we should abandon everything Mexican, our language, religion, and culture, and become totally Anglicized. It seemed to them that only a complete assimilation to the ways of the dominant would liberate us from the darkness of ignorance and the shackles of oppression. Movements of liberation were in the air everywhere, but there was a lot of disagreement as to what liberation meant and what the new life of freedom would be. I can well imagine that many similar questions went through Jesus' mind while working in Galilee and joining in the conversations of the people.

I myself was in the midst of these movements but was quite confused as to which was the right one. Should we just assimilate completely and try to wipe out all our Mexican background, maybe keeping just a few of the externals like Mariachi music and Mexican food? Or should we just acculturate, that is accommodate externally while maintaining our Mexican soul? Or even to the other extreme, should we reject everything of Anglo culture and seek to revive the ancient Mexican culture, even purified of the Spanish influence that came in with the conquest of 1521? For some, the only way was to purify ourselves of all foreign influence and reclaim the purity of our ancient ancestral ways of the natives of this land. These were not just ideas or theories; they were passionate convictions that inflamed these liberation movements but kept our own people divided.

In the very hopes and struggles for liberation of an oppressed and colonized people, can we not see and appreciate the various expectations of Messianic redemption at the time of Jesus? Everyone wanted it and longed for redemption, but there was little agreement as to just what it would be. Would anyone be able to bring the people out of this confusion and truly win liberation for them? Can you imagine Jesus in the midst of such conflicts and tensions in Galilee or in Texas today? Would he join one of the parties, one of the *movimientos*? Can you not imagine Jesus struggling with similar issues, especially before his baptism but even throughout his life? Would he simply do his job quietly and ignore the movements of his people—"pues hágase la voluntad de Dios" ("let God's will be done")? Or was there something more he could do, something unexpected, something others had not thought about?

I had two very important pivotal moments in my search for understanding the true way to liberation. The first came in the discovery that Anglo-Mexican mestizaje was not a burden but a great gift. It was not something to be ashamed of; I'm neither just Mexican nor just American, but something wholly new to be enjoyed with grateful pride. We are neither one people nor another, but the proud and beautiful children of both. In our very bodies and spirit we share in the rich heritage of both. This indeed is a unique blessing. This recognition opened the way for a totally new way of seeing, thinking, and understanding.

The second came in the discovery that we could only convert from the pain and shame of "non-being" into the joy and pride of "new-being" in and through Jesus of Nazareth. It was in the very cultural-religious uniqueness of the Messianic life and identity of Jesus of Nazareth that we would find the true meaning of our life and our quest. Our particular situation of living in the "in-between" would give us new insights into life and the Messianic mission of Jesus the Galilean savior, while his own Messianic identity and salvific ways would truly be healing and liberating news for us.

A Mestizo Messiah: "Neither Jew nor Gentile"

Imagine Jesus growing up Mexican-American in a rural town in Texas. I suspect no one, not even his own family and relatives, would have expected anything special out of him. After all, the ordinary and expected way of life was for the young people to stay around and take up the menial jobs their parents left them. Advancement was not in the air; subservience, endurance, and conformity appeared to be the rule. There were a few crazy visionaries who occasionally aroused the hopes of the people for change and betterment, but they usually never amounted to much. It seemed that nothing good could come out of the Jews of Galilee or the Mexican-Americans of Texas.

Jesus came out of Galilee to offer new hope to the people, beginning with the poorest of the poor, the lame, the sick, the legally impure, and all who were marginal to society in some way. The outcasts would experience a new sense of identity and belonging when they followed Jesus. Did Jesus know he was to be the Messiah? Scholars do not agree, but it seems clear that some people saw him as such.

Even today, scholars cannot agree on just who Jesus was. Leaders saw him as a troublemaker, diabolically possessed, a blasphemer (Mark 3:21), and a friend of drunkards and sinners. Likewise, our Mexican American movement leaders were quickly labeled as troublemakers, un-American, and even communists. The dominant society always tries to discredit the prophets. The prophet's word is self-evident, so the only way to silence the prophet is to discredit or destroy him or her.

Jesus' own family was not enthusiastic about his mission. They thought he had gone crazy and needed to be put away. The novelty of his life and mission provoked enthusiasm among the masses and controversy among the elites. His ministry could easily bring repercussions and trouble for the people of his home area. Many of our movement leaders experienced a similar reaction. They were altogether too much, even for their own families and too complex to be understood even by many of their followers.

Growing up in this region of interacting ethnicities made Jesus appear as an ambiguous leader. His vision, inner power, and charisma attracted many faithful and enthusiastic followers—often the masses of the people and sometimes even foreigners. Yet even the most faithful ones often misunderstood him (Matthew 15:16, 16:22–23; Mark 7:18; 8:32–33); at the end most of them abandoned him (Matthew 27:56; Mark 14:50), and even at the final moment of the ascension they were still asking the wrong question (Acts 1:6). Only at the very end, after a time of prayer and the reception of the Spirit, would they began to understand what Jesus was truly about (Acts 1 and 2). The leaders of the people saw him as a troublemaker, diabolically possessed, a blasphemer (Mark 3:21), and a friend of drunkards and sinners (Matthew 11:19, Luke 7:34). Likewise, our Mexican-American movement leaders were frequently misunderstood by our own people and quickly labeled as troublemakers, un-American, and even communists by mainline society. In the beginnings of the movements in the 1960s and 1970s, even some of our own church leaders called us divisive and troublemakers because we were calling the church to be serious about what it was teaching. The dominant society always tries to discredit the prophets. The prophet's word is self-evident, so the only way to silence the prophet is to discredit or destroy him or her.

But the ambiguity of Jesus goes much deeper. I suspect this could be the cultural basis of his Messianic secret and the deepest basis of the very passionate opposition of his own Jewish leaders. It is possibly the reason modern-day scholars have so many varied opinions about him. Some say he was a Jewish eschatological prophet preaching about the imminent end of times. Others say he was a social revolutionary. Still for others he was a Cynic philosopher, and for others he was a Charismatic Jew. For some he was a magician, while for others he was a Jewish wise man in the great wisdom tradition of the Hebrew Scriptures. Some would even call him a Jewish Socrates. There are many other learned opinions, but they all agree he was a marginal Jew from Galilee of Gentiles, as brought out in the very title of John Meier's masterful work on the historical Jesus.

In many ways Jesus appears to be a Mestizo—never easily understood by the established ethnicities, always ambiguous, always somewhat of a mystery. Just who is such a person? By merely growing up in Galilee he would have assimilated many of the traits of the various ethnicities of the region. Yet what many see as a negative— "ethnic contamination"—Jesus would turn into a positive. The very fact that he grew up in multicultural Galilee gave him a very privileged perspective on life, cultures, and religion. None would be totally strange to him, yet he would appear strange to all of them. This is very much the reality of Mestizo life even today. It seems evident that he was a staunch Jew sharing in the Messianic hopes of his people and reclaiming the best of his Jewish traditions, often criticizing the tradition of his day in the very name of the authentic tradition of the ancestors! As such, he would have alienated the Hellenistic elites of Jerusalem while delighting his own people of the land who loved and cherished their ancient traditions.

But because he had grown up in a strongly Hellenistic milieu, the Greek stories and traditions had become part of his inner self as well. He would sometimes appear to act and speak like a Greek Cynic philosopher, thus alienating the masses and shocking even his own closest disciples. Yet, by interconnecting the two, he took the best of both beyond their own limits and offered something truly new.

It seems to me that this is very clear in the famous confession of Peter. Peter confesses Jesus to be the Messiah according to Jewish expectations, and Jesus praises him for this. But Jesus then goes on to clarify it in terms similar to those of a Greek hero, and Peter cannot comprehend this (Matthew 16:13-23, Mark 8:27-33).

I suspect that the deepest root of the ambiguity and mystery of Jesus and the very reason why he was so often misunderstood even by his closest followers was that he appeared as a Jewish Messiah–Greek hero. He would not be just one or the other, but a marvelous combination of both, thus opening the way for people of different ethnicities to relate to him as a Jewish Messiah (Matthew and Mark) and as savior of humanity (Luke). Exclusively neither, yet both in the flesh of the same person. Precisely as such, he was tearing down the deepest walls of division: ethnic-religious absolutism! No wonder the temple veil was ripped apart at the moment of his death (Matthew 27:51). No longer would ethnic religions sacralize the horrible divisions created by sinful humanity. His life and mission, very much like that of any Mestizo leader, would not be easy to appreciate by those accustomed to ethnic-religious absolutism and afraid of being "contaminated" by other ethnicities or religions. Thus Jesus and his movement would continue to be "a stumbling block to the Jews and folly to the Gentiles" (1 Corinthians 1:23). Yet in his very flesh he unites humanity:

> "For he is our peace, he who made both [Jew and all others] one and broke down the dividing wall of enmity, through his flesh, abolishing the law with its commandments and legal claims, that he might create in himself one new person in place of the two, thus establishing peace, and might reconcile both with God, in one body, through the cross, putting that enmity to death by it." (Ephesians 2:14-16)

Only a Mestizo who in the flesh was both a Messiah for the Jewish people and a saving hero for the Gentiles could accomplish such a task and bring peace to humanity. He would not only be the mediator between God and humanity, but even more fascinating, the mediator between peoples who had previously detested one another.

St. Augustine puts this beautifully in his commentary on Psalm 126: "The true peacemaker [Christ] brought together in himself two walls coming from different angles and himself became the corner-stone. One wall was formed of the circumcised believers and the other of the uncircumcised gentiles who had faith." Amazing! The very ethnic religious walls that had served to keep people apart, now in the very person of Jesus, become the walls of the new Temple that will be a home for all the peoples of the world, a womb for the birth of a new humanity, and a playground for the formation of new friendships.

If we are going to work for the authentic unity of all peoples, it cannot be by wiping anyone out in favor of another. This has been the way of sinful humanity and only leads to distrust, anger, and bloodshed; there is nothing more brutal than religious wars. Jesus made a tremendous breakthrough to the "either/or" impasse of humanity; it was so drastic that it would be quickly recognized as a new creation, and he is the first-born of the new creation! Only by so doing could he offer hope to all and not privilege one group over another. In his Galilean identity and redemptive breakthrough, he has enlightened our own Mexican-American mestizo identity and clarified the very essence of our own movements for liberation and belonging. Because we are both in one but exclusively neither, we can rise above the dividing walls of separation, celebrate our new identity, and work for the unity through love of all peoples. Out of the margins of belonging, we are called to work for a new unity of everyone: the stone rejected by the builders of civilizations becomes the cornerstone that will bring them together into a new edifice, the ultimate Temple of God's universal love.

I have no way of knowing when and how Jesus processed his mestizaje so as to convert it from an enslaving shame into a liberating mission, but I can well suspect that it was precisely in his prolonged periods of intense prayer in which he was seeking the will of God, his loving and intimate Father who makes the sunrise on the good and the bad alike (Matthew 5:45)—that is, on all the peoples of the world without exception. The prolonged prayer in the desert and his struggles with the ordinary temptations of the good people of this world served as a purification. It was the beginning of the many fascinating incidents that make up the corpus of the gospel narratives. Only through intense prayer can we break through the prisons of our own cultural-religious world. Critical thinking is important, but inspired intuition comes through prayer and contemplation.

It was in God's providence that these diverse peoples, all creatures of the same God, had come together in the Roman colony of Palestine. They were all human beings equally created in the image and likeness of God. It was just not right for people to oppose and despise each other. It was not right for people to be declared outcasts and impure simply because of the work they did or the condition of their life. It was not right for a few to enrich themselves at the cost of the exploitation and misery of the masses. This could not be a reflection of the God of love. I am sure that as a child he had enjoyed aspects of the lives of everyone in the region, for children do not respect the segregating barriers created by adults. His love of God and his intimacy with God as his loving Father gave him possibilities into humanity that others had not suspected or dared to imagine. He had received so much from so many; now it was time to bring others into the fold of the new humanity made up of all the peoples of the world, truly a new race, a fascinating new creation upon the face of the earth.

No wonder Jesus said "go to Galilee" (Matthew 28:10). And today San Antonio is one of the Galilees in the world where the new creation is erupting. As we reflect on the gospel stories out of our own experience, we can easily imagine Jesus being among us today. Through the cultural images of the gospels, the understanding of our own life, struggles, and mission takes on a surprisingly new and challenging meaning. Even today, and until the end of time, God will continue to be a God of incredible surprises, especially in the Galilees of today where we will continue to see Jesus among the marginal calling us by name to be his disciples.

~

Bibliography

Beattie, Tina. *Rediscovering Mary: Insights from the Gospels*. Liguori, Mo.: Triumph Books, 1995.

Betz, Hans Dieter. Jesus and the Cynics: Survey and Analysis of a Hypothesis. *Journal of Religion* 74, no. 4 (1994): 453-476.

Blumenthal, David R. Repentance and Forgiveness. *Cross Currents* 48, no. 1 (1998): 75-83.

Boff, Leonardo, and Virgil Elizondo, eds. *1492-1992: The Voice of the Victims*. Philadelphia: Trinity Press International, 1990.

Boff, Leonardo. *Jesus Christ Liberator: A Critical Christology for Our Time*. Maryknoll, N.Y.: Orbis Books, 1979.

Boff, Leonardo. *Sacraments of Life: Life of the Sacraments*. Translated by John Drury. Washington, D.C.: Pastoral Press, 1987.

Bonino, Jose Miguez. *Faces of Latin American Protestantism*. 1993 Carnahan Lectures. Translated by Eugene L. Stockwell. Grand Rapids, Mich.: W. B. Eerdmans, 1997.

Borg, Marcus J. *Jesus, a New Vision: The Spirit, Culture, and the Life of Discipleship*. San Francisco: Harper and Row, 1987.

Brown Douglas, Kelly. *The Black Christ*. The Bishop Henry McNeal Turner Studies in North American Black Religion; Volume 9. Maryknoll: Orbis Books, 1994.

Brown, Raymond E. *Death of the Messiah: From Gethsemane to the Grave*, vol. 1. New York: Doubleday, 1994.

Brown, Raymond. *The Birth of the Messiah: A Commentary on the Infancy Narratives in the Gospels of Matthew and Luke*, new updated ed. Garden City, N.Y.: Doubleday, 1993.

Cavadini, John C. *The Last Christology of the West: Adoptionism in Spain and Gaul, 785-820*. Philadelphia: University of Pennsylvania Press, 1993.

Collins, John J., and Sterling, Gregory E. *Hellenism in the Land of Israel*. Notre Dame, Ind.: Notre Dame Press, 2001.

Crossan, John Dominic. *The Historical Jesus: The Life of a Mediterranean Jewish Peasant*. San Francisco: Harper San Francisco, 1991.

Cunneen, Sally. *In Search of Mary: The Woman and the Symbol*. New York: Ballantine Books, 1996.

Daino, Peter. *Mary: Mother of Sorrows, Mother of Defiance*. Maryknoll, N.Y.: Orbis Books, 1993.

Del Castillo, José García. *La imagen es el mensaje*. Caracas: Ediciones Tripode: 1987.

DeMaris, Richard E. The Baptism of Jesus: A Ritual-Critical Approach. In *The Social Setting of Jesus and the Gospels*. Edited by Wolfgang Stegemann, Bruce J. Malina, and Gerd Theissen. Minneapolis: Fortress Press, 2002.

Dillenberger, Jane. *Style and Content in Christian Art: From the Catacombs to the Chapel Designed by Matisse at Vence, France*. New York: Abingdon Press, 1965.

Downing, F. Gerald. *Christ and the Cynics: Jesus and Other Radical Preachers in the First Century Tradition*. Sheffield, UK: JSOT Press, 1988.

Dunn, James D. G. *Jesus and the Spirit*. Grand Rapids, Mich.: W. B. Eerdmans, 1997.

Eddy, Paul Rhodes. Jesus as Diogenes? Reflections on the Cynic Jesus Thesis. *Journal of Biblical Literature* 115, no. 3 (1996): 449-469.

Elizondo, Virgil. *The Future Is Mestizo: Life Where Cultures Meet*. Boulder: University of Colorado Press, 2000.

Elizondo, Virgilio P., and Timothy Matovina. *San Fernando Cathedral: Soul of the City*. Maryknoll, N.Y.: Orbis Books, 1998.

Elizondo, Virgilio. *Galilean Journey*. Maryknoll, N.Y.: Orbis Books, 2000.

Elizondo, Virgilio. *Guadalupe, Mother of the New Creation*. Maryknoll, N.Y.: Orbis Books, 1997.

Elizondo, Virgilio. *The Way of the Cross: The Passion of Christ in the Americas*. Maryknoll, N.Y.: Orbis Books, 1992.

Emerson, Yancey, and Chai Kim. *United in Faith: The Multicultural Congregation as an Answer to the Problem of Race*. Oxford: Oxford University Press, 2003.

Endo, Shusaku. *A Life of Jesus*. Translated by Richard A. Schuchert. New York: Paulist Press, 1989.

Fiorenza, Elizabeth Schüssler. *Jesus and the Politics of Interpretation*. New York: Continuum, 2000.

Freyne, Sean. *Galilee, Jesus and the Gospels: Literary Approaches and Historical Investigations*. Minneapolis: Fortress Press, 1988.

Garcia-Rivera, Alejandro. *A Wounded Innocence: Sketches for a Theology of Art*. Collegeville, Minn.: Liturgical Press, 2003.

Gebara, Ivone, and Maria Clara Bingemer. *Mary, Mother of God, Mother of the Poor*. Maryknoll, N.Y.: Orbis Books, 1989.

Goizueta, Roberto S. *Caminemos con Jesús: Toward a Hispanic/Latino Theology of Accompaniment*. Maryknoll, N.Y.: Orbis Books, 1995.

Groody, Daniel G. *Border of Death, Valley of Life*. New York: Rowman & Littlefield, 2002.

Gutierrez, Gustavo. *On Job: God-Talk and the Suffering of the Innocent*. Maryknoll, N.Y.: Orbis Books, 1987.

Gutierrez, Gustavo. *We Drink from Our Own Wells: The Spiritual Journey of a People*. Maryknoll, N.Y.: Orbis Books, 1990.

Hendrickx, Herman. *The Resurrection Narratives of the Synoptic Gospels*. London: G. Chapman, 1984.

Hendrickx, Herman. *The Infancy Narratives*. London: G. Chapman, 1984.

Hendrickx, Herman. *The Passion Narratives of the Synoptic Gospels*. London: G. Chapman, 1984.

Hendrickx, Herman. *The Third Gospel for the Third World*. Collegeville, Minn.: Liturgical Press, 1984.

Hennessy, Anne. *The Galilee of Jesus*. Rome: Editrice Pontificia Universita Gregoriana, 1994.

Hertig, Paul. The Multi-ethnic Journeys of Jesus in Matthew: Margin-Center Dynamics. *Missiology: An International Review* 31, no. 1 (1998): 23-35.

Herzog, William R. *Jesus, Justice, and the Reign of God: A Ministry of Liberation*. Louisville, Ky.: Westminster John Knox Press, 2000.

Horsley, Richard A. *Archaeology, History and Society in Galilee*. Harrisburg, Pa.: Trinity Press International, 2000.

Horsley, Richard A. *Galilee: History, Politics, People*. Harrisburg, Pa.: Trinity Press International, 1997.

Jeremias, Joachim. *Jerusalem in the Time of Jesus: An Investigation into Economic and Social Conditions during the New Testament Period*. Philadelphia: Fortress Press, 1969.

John Paul II. Encyclical Letter *Redemptor Hominis*. Rome, 1979.

Johnson, Elizabeth A. *Truly Our Sister: A Theology of Mary in the Communion of Saints*. New York: Continuum, 2003.

Jonge, Marinus de. *Christology in Context: The Earliest Christian Response to Jesus*. Philadelphia: Westminster Press, 1988.

Just, Arthur A. *Ongoing Feast*. Collegeville, Minn.: Liturgical Press, 1993.

Küster, Volker. *The Many Faces of Jesus Christ*. Maryknoll, N.Y.: Orbis Books, 1999.

Lampman, Lisa Barnes. *God and the Victim: Theological Reflections on Evil, Victimization, Justice and Forgiveness*. Washington D.C.: Neighbors Who Care, 1999.

Latourelle, Rene. *Finding Jesus through the Gospels: History and Hermeneutics*. New York: Alba House, 1978.

Laurentin, Rene. *Structure et theologie de Luc I-II*. Paris: Etudes Bibliques, 1957.

Linskins, John. *Christ Liberator of the Poor: Secularity, Wealth, and Poverty in the Gospel of St. Luke*. Scripture Today Series Volume 4. San Antonio: Mexican American Cultural Center, 1976.

MacArthur, John F. *Forgiveness*. Wheaton, Ill.: Crossway Books, 1998.

Malina, Bruce J. *The New Testament World: Insights from Cultural Anthropology*. Louisville, Ky.: Westminster John Knox Press, 2001.

Mateos, Juan, and F. Camacho. *El Evangelio de Mateo*. Madrid: Ediciones Cristiandad, 1981.

Matovina, Timothy, and Gary Riebe-Estrella. *Horizons of the Sacred: Mexican Tradition in U.S. Catholicism*. Ithaca, N.Y.: Cornell University Press, 2002.

McDonnell, Kilian. The Baptism of Jesus in the Jordan and the Descent into Hell. *Worship* 69, no. 2 (2001): 98-109.

Meier, John P. *A Marginal Jew: Rethinking the Historical Jesus. Vol. 2, Mentor Message, and Miracles*. Doubleday, 1994.

Meier, John P. *A Marginal Jew: Rethinking the Historical Jesus. Vol. 1, The Roots of the Problem and the Person*. New York: Doubleday, 1991.

Menni, Albert. *The Colonizer and the Colonized*. Boston: Beacon Press, 1972.

Meyers, Eric M., ed. *Galilee through the Centuries: Confluence of Cultures*. Duke Judaic Studies Series, vol. 1. Winona Lake, Ind.: Eisenbrauns, 1999.

Mitchell, Margaret M. *Social World of the First Christians*. Minneapolis: Augsburg Fortress, 1995.

Gonzalez-Faus, Jose Ignacio. *Acceso a Jésus*. Madrid: Ediciones Sigueme, 1979.

Moltman, Jurgen. *The Crucified God: The Cross of Christ as the Foundation and Criticism of Christian Theology*. New York: Harper and Row, 1974.

Neyrey, Jerome H. *Honor and Shame in the Gospel of Matthew*. Louisville, Ky.: Westminster John Knox Press, 1998.

Nolan, Albert. *Jesus before Christianity*. Maryknoll, N.Y.: Orbis Books, 1992.

O'Gorman, Bob, and Faulker, Mary. Why Do We Say Mary Was 'Ever Virgin? *U.S. Catholic* 66, no. 5 (2001): 38.

Pallares, José Cardenas. *A Poor Man Called Jesus: Reflections on the Gospel of Mark*. Maryknoll, N.Y.: Orbis Books, 1986.

Paul VI. Apostolic Letter on Evangelization *Evangeli Nutiandi*. Rome, December 8, 1975.

Peelman, Achiel. *Christ Is a Native American*. Maryknoll, N.Y.: Orbis Books, 1995.

Pelikan, Jaroslav. *Jesus through the Centuries: His Place in the History of Culture*. New York: Perennial Library, 1987.

Pelikan, Jaroslav. *Mary through the Centuries: Her Place in the History of Culture*. New Haven, Conn.: Yale University Press, 1996.

Perrin, Norman. *Rediscovering the Teaching of Jesus*. New York: Harper and Row, 1976.

Powell, Mark Allan. *Jesus as a Figure in History: How Modern Historians View the Man from Galilee*. Louisville, Ky.: Westminster John Knox Press, 1998.

Riley, Gregory J. *One Jesus, Many Christs: How Jesus Inspired Not Only One Christianity, But Many: The Truth About Christian Origins*. San Francisco: Harper San Francisco, 1997.

Sanders, E. P. *The Historical Figure of Jesus*. London: Penguin, 1993.

Schaberg, Jane. *The Illegitimacy of Jesus: A Feminist Theological Interpretation of the Infancy Narratives*. New York: Crossroad, 1990.

Schmithals, Walter. *Theology of the First Christians*. Louisville, Ky.: Westminster John Knox Press, 1997.

Schneiders, Sandra M. *Written That You May Believe: Encountering Jesus in the Fourth Gospel*. New York: Crossroad, 1999.

Schökel, Luis Alonso. *A Manual of Hermeneutics*. The Bible Seminar Series. Translated by Liliana M. Rosa. Further editing by Brook W. R. Pearson. Sheffield: Sheffield Academic Press, 1998.

Schökel, Luis Alonso. *The Inspired Word: Scripture in the Light of Language and Literature*. New York: Herder and Herder, 1965.

Schökel, Luis Alonso. *The Literary Language of the Bible: The Collected Essays of Luis Alonso Schökel*. Bibal Collected Essays, vol. 3. N. Richland Hills, Tex.: D & F Scott, 2001.

Schottroff, Luise, and Wolfgang Stegeman. *Jesus and the Hope of the Poor*. Maryknoll, N.Y.: Orbis Books, 1986.

Schreiter, Robert J., ed. *Faces of Jesus in Africa*. Maryknoll, N.Y.: Orbis Books, 1991.

Segovia, Fernando F. *Decolonizing Biblical Studies: A View from the Margins*. Maryknoll, N.Y.: Orbis Books, 2000.

Segovia, Fernando F. *Interpreting beyond Borders*. Sheffield: Sheffield Academic Press, 2000.

Senior, Donald. *Jesus, A Gospel Portrait*. Dayton: Pflaum Publishers, 1975.

Soares-Prabhu, George M., and Francis Xavier D'Sa, ed. *Innocence*. Maryknoll, N.Y.: Orbis Books, 2003.

Soares-Prabhu, George M., and Francis Xavier D'Sa, ed. *The Dharma of Jesus*. Maryknoll, N.Y.: Orbis Books, 2003.

Soares-Prabhu, George M., and Francis Xavier D'Sa, ed. *The Praxis of Jesus*. Maryknoll, N.Y.: Orbis Books, 2003.

Sobrino, Jon. *Christology at the Crossroads: Aa Latin American Approach*. Maryknoll, N.Y.: Orbis Books, 1978.

Sobrino, Jon. *Jesus the Liberator: A Historical-Theological View*. Maryknoll, N.Y.: Orbis Books, 1993.

Sölle, Dorothee. *The Strength of the Weak: Toward a Christian Feminist Identity*. Translated by Robert and Rita Kimber. Philadelphia: Westminster Press, 1984.

Sugirtharajah, R. S., ed. *Asian Faces of Jesus*. Maryknoll, N.Y.: Orbis Books, 1993.

Theissen, Gerd, and Annette Merz. *The Historical Jesus: A Comprehensive Guide*. Minneapolis: Fortress Press, 1998.

Theissen, Gerd. *The Shadow of the Galilean: The Quest of the Historical Jesus in Narrative Form*. Philadelphia: Fortress Press, 1987.

Third General Conference of Latin American Bishops, convened at Puebla, Mexico, January 1979. Discourse to the opening session of the Puebla Meeting: Final Documents. In *Puebla and Beyond*. Edited by John Eagleson and Philip Scharper. Maryknoll, N.Y.: Orbis Books, 1979.

Thurman, Howard. *Jesus and the Disinherited*. Boston: Becon Press, 1996.

Van Aarde, Andries. *Fatherless in Galilee: Jesus as a Child of God*. Harrisburg, Pa.: Trinity Press International, 2001.

Van Voorst, Robert E. *Jesus Outside the New Testament: An Introduction to the Ancient Evidence, Studying the Historical Jesus*. Grand Rapids, Mich.: W.B. Eerdmans, 2000.

Wink, Walter. *Engaging the Powers: Discernment and Resistance in a World of Domination*. Minneapolis: Fortress Press, 1992.

Wink, Walter. *John the Baptist in the Gospel Tradition*. London: Cambridge University Press, 1968.

Wink, Walter. *The Human Being: Jesus and the Enigma of the Son of the Man*. Minneapolis: Fortress Press, 2002.

Index

~

About the Author

Virgilio Elizondo, cited by *Time* magazine as one of the nation's spiritual innovators for the third millennium, is professor of pastoral theology at the Mexican American Cultural Center and at the University of Notre Dame, producer at Catholic Television of San Antonio, and vicar at St. Rose of Lima Parish in San Antonio, Texas. He is the author of *The Human Quest, Christianity and Culture, Virgen y Madre, La Morenita: Evangelizer of the Americas, Galilean Journey: The Mexican American Promise, The Future Is Mestizo: Life Where Cultures Meet, Guadalupe: Mother of the New Creation, Mestizo Worship* (with Timothy Matovina), *San Fernando Cathedral: Soul of the City* (with Timothy Matovina), *A Retreat with Our Lady of Guadalupe and Juan Diego*, and *The Way of the Cross: The Passion of Christ in the Americas.*